ROUTLEDGE LIBRARY EDITIONS:
ALCOHOL AND ALCOHOLISM

Volume 10

I0095337

ALCOHOLISM
IN PERSPECTIVE

ALCOHOLISM IN PERSPECTIVE

Edited by
MARCUS GRANT
AND
PAUL GWINNER

R Routledge
Taylor & Francis Group

LONDON AND NEW YORK

First published in 1979 by Croom Helm

This edition first published in 2024
by Routledge
4 Park Square, Milton Park, Abingdon, Oxon OX14 4RN

and by Routledge
605 Third Avenue, New York, NY 10158

Routledge is an imprint of the Taylor & Francis Group, an informa business

British Library Cataloguing in Publication Data
A catalogue record for this book is available from the British Library

ISBN: 978-1-032-59082-0 (Set)
ISBN: 978-1-032-61690-2 (Volume 10) (hbk)
ISBN: 978-1-032-61702-2 (Volume 10) (pbk)
ISBN: 978-1-032-61698-8 (Volume 10) (ebk)

DOI: 10.4324/9781032616988

Publisher's Note
The publisher has gone to great lengths to ensure the quality of this reprint but points out that some imperfections in the original copies may be apparent.

Disclaimer
The publisher has made every effort to trace copyright holders and would welcome correspondence from those they have been unable to trace.

ALCOHOLISM IN PERSPECTIVE

Edited by
MARCUS GRANT and PAUL GWINNER

CROOM HELM LONDON

© 1979 Marcus Grant and Paul Gwinner
Croom Helm Ltd, 2-10 St John's Road, London SW11
ISBN 0-85664-790-X (Hb)
ISBN 0-85664-842-6 (Pb)

Printed in Great Britain by
Biddles Ltd, Guildford, Surrey

CONTENTS

ALCOHOLISM IN PERSPECTIVE

1 INTRODUCTION

Marcus Grant & Paul Gwinner

In the past few years, a shift of emphasis has been taking place in the alcoholism field which has led to some fundamental changes in central concepts. Alcoholism was formerly conceptualised as a categorical and discrete condition affecting a distinct group of people who were presumed to suffer from an 'illness' of uncertain (but presumably bio-chemically determined) aetiology. The shift of emphasis has been towards a new dimensional model of drinking behaviour. In this dimensional model, alcoholism is conceptualised as being at the extreme of the drinking continuum so that it emerges from normal drinking behaviour rather than being artificially separated from it. The dimensional model also views alcoholism more as a syndrome and less as a discrete condition. The change of emphasis has had the effect, therefore, of obliterating the simplistic distinction between alcoholic and non-alcoholic subjects and of recognising the wide range of alcohol-related disabilities which manifest themselves in the world today.

This book represents an attempt to look afresh at the subject of alcoholism, from the standpoint of this changing perspective. It is all the more necessary because the general change in emphasis has been paralleled by a number of individual changes which have occurred within particular professional approaches to the problem, at both a theoretical and a practical level. These changes have not been confined to basic concepts determining the nature of alcoholism but have also radically affected treatment philosophy. It is these shifts in emphasis which form the contextual foundation of this book.

The contributors emerge from different disciplines and present a multi-disciplinary approach of widely differing perspectives. This accurately reflects pragmatic actuality as the alcoholism field is no longer dominated by a single professional group. The contributors' commonality is firmly vested in patient and client contact, to which they bring diverse bodies of theoretical knowledge.

In this book we have attempted to integrate theory and practice and to acknowledge the important symbiotic relationship which characterises these two phenomena, particularly at a time of renaissance, such as currently characterises the alcoholism field. The aim of the book is to make accessible to all those who may be involved in dealing with problems related to alcohol and alcoholism the special insights which emerge from a range of different perspectives. Thus, contributions have been sought which represent individual distillations of particular areas of knowledge but which also combine to produce a fresh and holistic view of alcoholism today.

This book is the first to be produced jointly by Croom Helm and the Alcohol Education Centre, although a previous Croom Helm volume, *Alcoholism: New Knowledge and New Responses* (edited by Griffith Edwards and Marcus Grant), was based upon a conference organised by the Alcohol Education Centre and the Institute of Psychiatry, University of London. It is hoped that a number of other books will be produced jointly by Croom Helm and the Alcohol Education Centre. Future subjects are likely to include Alcoholism and the Family, Alcohol and Work, Legal Aspects of Alcohol Problems (which are not discussed in the present publication) and other special topics within the general subject.

The Alcohol Education Centre is an independent organisation whose function is to provide education and training for all those who work with the problems resulting from alcohol abuse. It runs a wide range of conferences, seminars and courses. Further information about its activities can be obtained from The Alcohol Education Centre, The Maudsley Hospital, 99 Denmark Hill, London SE5 8AZ.

The editors of this book would like to acknowledge the helpful guidance received from the Alcohol Education Centre's Publications Working Group, comprising Dr D.L. Davies, Miss Linda Hunt, Dr Jim Orford, Dr Martin Plant and Dr Rodney Wilkins. A particular debt of gratitude is due to Miss Beryl Skinner for her superb patience in tracking down errant references and her unfailing attention to detail in every aspect of preparing the typescript for publication. Thanks is also due to Mrs Vivienne Henry who prepared the index.

This book will not provide readers with an off-the-peg set of answers on how to deal with alcoholics. What the book attempts to do is to put alcoholism into perspective at a time when it is easy to make false assumptions. It also attempts to offer readers practical guidelines which will help them understand the theory and practices of their own profession within a broader and more rational context.

2 THE PHYSIOLOGY OF ALCOHOL

G.K. Shaw

The major intoxicant of the beers, wines and spirits that we drink is a clear, colourless, somewhat volatile liquid, ethyl alcohol. Ethyl alcohol is one of a series of alcohols, which are relatively simple organic chemical substances made up of carbon, oxygen and hydrogen in various proportions. It is formed by the action of the cells of the yeast plant on various fruit juices and thus it occurs naturally.

This process, called fermentation, is the basis of the commercial production of wines and beers. Using this method, drinks containing alcohol up to a limit of 15 per cent by volume may be produced. At about this strength, the concentration of alcohol kills off the yeast cells, effectively preventing further alcohol production. These relatively weak brews may be further concentrated by distillation to produce strong spirits. Spirits may be drunk on their own or they may be used to fortify (increase the alcoholic strength of) wines, thereby producing the so-called fortified wines, such as sherry or port.

These wines, beers and spirits have characteristic differences in colour, taste and smell but what is important for the student of alcoholism is that they all contain, in different proportions, the active substance ethyl alcohol. The various drinks and their approximate strengths expressed as a percentage of pure alcohol by volume are listed in Table 2.1.

Table 2.1: Approximate Strength of Various Drinks (expressed as % of alcohol by volume)

Beverage	% alcohol by volume
Beer and ale	4-8
Table wine	11-14
Fortified wine (sherry, port, etc.)	18-23
Spirits (whisky, rum, brandy, etc.)	35-50

In the United Kingdom the strength of alcoholic drinks is often expressed in degrees of proof spirit rather than as a percentage of pure alcohol. This measure is derived from the old method of 'proving' that an alcoholic drink was up to strength by mixing it with a little gunpowder and attempting to ignite it. If the drink contained a minium of 49 per cent of alcohol by weight or 57 per cent of alcohol by volume then the mixture could be lit. If, however, the alcoholic content was less than that, then it could not. This concentration of alcohol was therefore taken to be 'proof spirit' or 100° proof. As a rough guide, therefore, the strength of any alcoholic drink given in UK degrees proof can be converted into percentage of alcohol by volume, by dividing by two the degrees of proof. So that, for example, 70° proof whisky contains approximately 35 per cent of alcohol by volume.

Ethyl alcohol has a number of important physio-chemical properties. It mixes freely with water in any proportion, so that once in the body it is rapidly dispersed throughout all the tissue fluids and thus has ready access to all organs. It is also soluble in fat and readily infiltrates the cells of the central nervous system which are themselves rich in fat. In this way alcohol exerts important early effects on thinking, feeling and behaviour.

Alcohol is unusual in that it is both a drug (indeed the most commonly used drug in the world) and a foodstuff. As a food it is a rich source of energy, yielding 7cals/gm of alcohol. It therefore yields more energy than an equivalent amount of protein or carbohydrate and only slightly less energy than an equivalent amount of fat. Furthermore, since it does not require to be digested, but is taken up unchanged from the stomach to the bloodstream, it is a rapid source of energy. It is nevertheless a poor food since it lacks proteins, vitamins and other essential nutrients.

Indeed if alcohol is taken in excess, it is potent cause of malnutrition. Firstly, since it is a rich source of calories, if a full diet is taken it disturbs the usual balance between carbohydrate, protein and fat and this may have deleterious consequences. More usually, of course, it discourages the taking of a full diet. Secondly, alcohol causes gastritis, a chronic inflammatory thickening of the stomach lining which lessens that organ's ability to absorb nutrients from the diet. Thirdly, the presence of alcohol in the body interferes with the utilisation, at the cellular level, of certain vitamins essential to health. Lastly, there is the possibility that taking alcohol in excess increases the need for certain nutrients essential for its breakdown, thus exacerbating any existing deficiency (Thomson, 1978).

Absorption, Metabolism and Excretion of Alcohol

Alcohol has no major effect on the body (with the exception of the gastritis earlier commented on) until it is absorbed, that is to say,

transported from the stomach to the bloodstream. Once in the bloodstream, it is rapidly distributed to all the organs of the body, but
many factors alter the rate at which it is absorbed.

Of prime importance here is the fact that alcohol is absorbed
rapidly and completely from the small intestine but relatively slowly
from the stomach. It follows that factors which delay the onward
transmission of alcohol from the stomach to the small intestine will
slow the rate of absorption, and that factors which hasten the passage
of alcohol from the stomach to the small intestine will accelerate the
rate of absorption. This probably explains the well-known fact that
alcohol is better tolerated on a full stomach than on an empty one.
Mixing food with alcohol delays, in a simple mechanical way, the
passage of alcohol to the small intestine, thus reducing the rate of
absorption. It matters little what type of food is taken, nor, providing
the intervals are not unduly prolonged, whether the food is taken
before, with, or after the alcohol.

The type of alcoholic beverage has a slight effect. Pure alcohol is
taken up most rapidly of all and spirits more rapidly than beer,
presumably reflecting the importance of substances other than
alcohol insofar as absorption rates are concerned. The strength of the
drink is also important, absorption taking place most rapidly at concen-
trations between 15-30 per cent of alcohol. Below that strength, the
concentration gradient between the stomach contents and the
bloodstream does not favour rapid diffusion; above that level, there is
a tendency for the stomach lining to be irritated with the production of
a sticky mucous which delays absorption and there is a further tendency
for the valve linking the stomach to the small intestine, the pylorus, to
go into spasm, thereby delaying the passage of alcohol to the small
intestine, where it would be more more rapidly absorbed.

Drugs which interfere with gastric mobility, and there are many such,
will either hasten or delay the rates of absorption. Temperature also has
a slight effect, warm alcohol being absorbed more rapidly than cold
alcohol.

Whatever the factors altering the rates of absorption, alcohol is in
fact absorbed quite quickly and maximum blood levels are reached
1-1½ hours after consumption. In a man of average size it has been
estimated that a measure of whisky, a glass of wine, a glass of port or
half a pint of beer (these measures all contain approximately the same
amount of ethyl alcohol), will generate a rise in the blood alcohol level
of 15 mg of alcohol/100 ml of blood. It would be unwise, however, for
those wishing to remain within legal limits, as far as driving is concerned,

to rely too heavily on this equation, since as we have already noted, many factors will influence absorption rates. There is, furthermore, great variation between individuals in this respect, and it is known that even if the *same* individual takes identical amounts of alcohol on two apparently similar drinking occasions, the resulting blood alcohol levels may differ by as much as twofold.

Only a small portion, some 5 per cent of the alcohol in the bloodstream is got rid of unaltered in the urine or in the breath. The major portion is broken down in the body.

The first stage in the breakdown process occurs mainly in the liver and sees alcohol broken down to acetaldehyde.

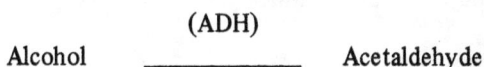

(ADH)

Alcohol ——————— Acetaldehyde

This process is facilitated by an enzyme called alcohol dehydrogenase (ADH) and proceeds at a constant rate which is not increased however much alcohol there is in the bloodstream in need of breaking down. In an average person the rate of breakdown is such as to reduce the blood alcohol level by 15 mg/100 ml blood/hour. The chemically dependent alcoholic is, in fact, capable of breaking down alcohol more rapidly than this, perhaps up to twice as fast. How this is achieved is unclear but it is suggested that alcoholics press into service another enzyme, catalase, and another system also located in the liver, the microsomal ethanol oxidising system, and in this way increase their ability to break down alcohol by as much as 100 per cent.

A drug which would speed up the breakdown of alcohol would have a definite medical value. It would enable us rapidly to sober up the dangerously intoxicated individual and it would help to solve a problem with which casualty officers have to contend. Quite often a man may be brought to the casualty department in coma and smelling of alcohol. It is, of course, difficult to know to what extent the alcohol is contributing to the coma and a 'sobering-up' drug would rapidly clarify the situation. Many drugs have been tried but only one, fructose, a sugar, has been found to have any merit. If given intravenously in fairly generous amounts, it has been found to increase the rate of breakdown of alcohol by as much as 80 per cent. Unfortunately, it also has disadvantages so that its practical value is limited.

The second stage in the breakdown of alcohol is the conversion of acetaldehyde to acetate. Fortunately this reaction proceeds rapidly since acetaldehyde is a toxic substance and produces very unpleasant symptoms if present in quantity in the body. This fact forms the basis for the use of drugs such as Antabuse and Abstem as a deterrent to drinking in the alcoholic. These drugs block the breakdown of acetaldehyde. In consequence, if a person taking one of these drugs also takes a drink, acetaldehyde builds up in the body, causing flushing of the skin, nausea and perhaps vomiting, feelings of uneasiness and if the reaction is sufficiently severe, collapse with breathlessness and chest pain. Anyone taking these drugs is, of course, carefully instructed that they must not drink while taking the drug.

The final stage in the breakdown sees acetate converted to a gas, carbon dioxide and water, during which process a good deal of energy is liberated.

The Effects of Alcohol

Alcohol is a member of that group of depressant drugs which includes the volatile anaesthetics. It has many properties in common with these drugs and it is itself an anaesthetic and a pain killer. It is, however, no longer made use of in that capacity, since there is little margin between the dose level at which full anaethesia is produced and the dose at which the brain centre responsible for respiration is dangerously depressed with the risk of respiratory arrest.

Alcohol produces its effect on the body and on behaviour in different ways. Some effects follow a direct toxic effect of alcohol or some of its breakdown products on the cells of the central nervous system and the cells of the liver. A further group of symptoms, collectively known as withdrawal symptoms, arise when the physically dependent alcoholic is deprived of alcohol. Many of the more chronic effects are produced indirectly either by nutritional deficiency or as a secondary consequence of damage to important body organs, particularly the liver.

The study of these effects of alcohol is a complex matter, since many factors alter the response to alcohol. Responses at different dose levels may be quite contradictory, and the effects of acute administration are often at variance with the effect of chronic administration. Whether the blood level has risen quickly or slowly, and how long the rise has been sustained, are both factors which considerably modify the effect. Effects in the naive subject are, of course, very different from effects in the alcohol sophisticate.

It is convenient to consider the immediate effects of alcohol separately from its longer term effects.

Immediate Effects

The well-known immediate consequence of drinking alcohol is acute intoxication. In general, the degree of intoxication parallels the blood alcohol level, but of course, individuals vary greatly in their ability to 'tolerate' alcohol. It may also be assumed that the more rapidly the blood alcohol level has risen, and the shorter the period of time through which it has been sustained, the greater will be the behavioural disruption. The speed of drinking, the total dose consumed and the various factors, earlier commented on, which modify rates of absorption, are all therefore important determinants of the degree of intoxication.

At low dose levels, alcohol has a slight stimulating effect on the brain (Kalant, 1975), but this is soon overtaken by a depressant action which affects early areas of the brain responsible for the integration and control of complex thinking, feeling and behaviour.

The environmental situation is important, and in lively company one may expect disinhibited behaviour.The drinker becomes less self-conscious, more talkative, and less discreet. Judgement and restraint are impaired and there is loss of emotional control. The skin is flushed and warm and the heart rate increased. Muscular control is impaired early and progressively deteriorates as the blood level rises.

At higher dose levels, thinking becomes slow and superficial and learning and retention of information become faulty. Less attention is paid to stimuli from without and within so that feelings, for example, of hunger or pain are ignored, sometimes with dire consequences. In the case of environmental stimuli, events at the periphery are progressively ignored until only the immediate situation is given attention. At low dose levels, alcohol may sometimes relieve feelings of anxiety and depression, but at higher levels there is a distinct tendency for these feelings to be worsened. Table 2.2 charts the approximate correlations between blood alcohol level and behaviour.

The fact that this state of impaired physical, mental and emotional functioning is usually accompanied by increased feelings of wellbeing and confidence, explains alcohol's unique contribution to accidents of many kinds.

Forgetfulness of the events of a drinking bout producing extreme drunkenness is, of course, to be expected since it is clear that information is not being registered and that it will not therefore be recalled at a later date. Sometimes, however, memory disturbance follows a drinking bout which has seemingly produced little outward disturbance of behaviour. The subject seems well able to carry on a conversation and

Table 2.2: Approximate Correlations Between Blood Alcohol Level and Behaviour

Blood alcohol level	Behaviour
30 mg/100 ml	Mild feelings of wellbeing
50 mg/100 ml	Slight unsteadiness
	Nystagmus probable
100 mg/100 ml	Obvious ataxia
	Nystagmus present
300 mg/100 ml	Stuporose
500 mg/100 ml	Coma and death

may be able to cope relatively well with such complex activities as driving a car. The following morning, however, his memory is blank and no amount of effort will enable him to recall the events of the previous night. This alarming experience is known as the alcoholic 'blackout' or amnesic episode.

In fact, however, this experience is not confined to alcoholics and some have suggested that 30-40 per cent of young males will have experienced one or more such episodes. Experimental studies by Goodwin *et al.* (1969), amongst others, have made it clear that despite the apparently normal behaviour during the amnesic episode, the sufferer is unable to take in information or to recall it a few minutes later. He is therefore to some extent operating in an automatic fashion. This type of reaction is associated with a style of heavy drinking, particularly of spirits, which causes a rapid rise in the blood alcohol level. Of itself, it does not, as is often feared, betoken the onset of dementia; nonetheless it is an indication that the drinking style is unhealthy and potentially dangerous.

Long-term Effects of Alcohol

The development of tolerance and dependence are two important effects of the chronic administration of alcohol. Tolerance is that familiar phenomenon whereby increased experience of alcohol necessitates more of the drug to produce the same effect. This tolerance reaches impressive levels in the alcoholic and Mello and Mendelson (1970) have reported that most alcoholics can drink 30 oz of whisky daily without signs of gross intoxication. This degree of tolerance is not adequately explained by the alcoholic's enhanced ability to break down alcohol. Furthermore, acute tolerance may be seen after a single administration of alcohol, in the sense that disturbance at any given level of blood alcohol is always more pronounced

when the blood level is rising than it is when the blood level is falling.
It would seem that some adaptive process involving the cerbral neurones
is at work.

Contrary to popular belief, tolerance to alcohol develops quite
rapidly, after only a week or two of chronic exposure to the drug, and
after a short period of abstinence, tolerance rapidly fades. Once tolerance has been acquired, however, it is rapidly reacquired on further
exposure to the drug, which is why bout drinking alcoholics appear to
retain tolerance from one bout to the next.

Definitional problems of dependence are dealt with in Chapter 5. In
practical terms, however, the presence of dependence is recognised
either when there is evidence that a person's thinking is dominated by
thoughts of alcohol and how to obtain it, and when he is no longer able
to choose whether or not to have a drink, but feels that he must have
one, or by the development of an abstinence syndrome when alcohol is
stopped after a period of chronic administration.

It can no longer be doubted that alcohol is a drug capable of causing
physical dependence and it seems probable that anyone will become
dependent if only they drink enough. There are interesting experimental
studies touching on these matters, notably those of Isbell *et al.* (1955)
and Mendelson and his colleagues (1964). More recent epidemiological
work suggests that long continued drinking at a level of 150 ml of
alcohol daily, that is the equivalent of approximately five pints of beer
or five double whiskies, carries with it the distinct risk of developing
physical dependence.

The mode of action of physical dependence is not understood but
since 1970 there has been active interest in a possible pharmacological
link with opiate dependence. Two groups of investigators, Davis
and Walsh (1970) and Cohen and Collins (1970), reported the formation
of tetrahydroisoquinoline alkaloids as a consequence of alcohol
metabolism. The significance of this is that these alkaloids are very
similar to morphine. The recent demonstration of the presence in
man of naturally occurring opiate-like substance called enkaphalins and
the demonstration of opiate receptors in the brain to which these
substances bind, has added strength to the view that alcohol
dependency is in some way linked to changes induced in these brain
areas.

Whatever the mechanism of physical dependency, it is a potent
cause of continued drinking in the alcoholic who drinks, inter alia, in
order to keep at bay unpleasant symptoms of abstinence. As in the case
of tolerance, physical dependency passes off quite rapidly after a period

of abstinence, but is quickly reacquired in the event of further episodes of heavy drinking.

The usual symptoms of withdrawal in the physically dependent alcoholic are tremulousness, convulsions and delirium. The situation is complicated, however, since there can be no doubt that these 'withdrawal' symptoms may also occur in the alcoholic whilst he continues to drink. In at least a third of the cases where delirium occurs, the alcoholic is still drinking. Sometimes illnesses or infections are incriminated, sometimes an actual increase in the amount drunk is noted. It seems therefore that this group of symptoms represent a failure of the body's adaptive mechanism to alcohol and that at a minimum this failure may be brought about by intercurrent illness, by abrupt cessation of drinking or by drinking at an overwhelming level.

Tremulousness is the commonest sympton and occurs early, a few hours after stopping drinking. It is therefore a matter of everyday experience for the severely physically dependent alcoholic. It reaches peak severity 6-12 hours after stopping drinking and the tremor may be so severe that to dress or to carry a glass to the lips become major obstacles to be overcome. Usually the tremor is accompanied by nausea, weakness, feelings of apprehension and a tendency to startle readily. The 'relief' drinking usually resorted to in order to deal with this syndrome is an important indicator of the presence of physical dependence.

Alcohol may precipitate fits in the epileptic, in which event the fit tends to occur during the drinking episode. Withdrawal fits, however, usually occur 13-24 hours after the last drink and fits which occur later than 48 hours after the last drink should always prompt a search for an alternative cause. Withdrawal fits are usually single fits or at the most a few fits spread over an hour or two. They usually respond to routine treatment with anticonvulsants which need not be continued for longer than a few days.

The most severe form of withdrawal symptom is delirium tremens and it is a life-threatening condition requiring specialised care. Classically it develops three days after stopping drinking. It may develop suddenly or may be ushered in by a few nights of broken sleep disturbed by nightmares. As the full blown syndrome develops, the physical picture is dominated by coarse persistent tremulousness of the hands, head and trunk, by extreme restlessness and by agitated activity. The patient perspires freely, the pulse is rapid and the temperature is likely to be slight raised.

Mentally the patient is confused. He does not know where he is, nor what day it is and he misidentifies people. He is hallucinated, often seeing small fast-moving terrifying animals, and hearing threatening voices. Usually the emotional state is one of fear and distress. In response to these frightening and threatening experiences, aggressive or suicidal behaviour may emerge. For this reason and in order to prevent the patient exhausing himself, treatment in hospital is desirable. Usually the response to treatment is satisfactory but occasionally deaths occur.

In addition to producing the adaptive changes – tolerance and dependence – alcohol has long term effects on many of the organs of the body, notably the brain, the liver and the heart.

In the case of the brain, many rare neurological syndromes (Shaw, 1978) may be found in which the most important is a specialised type of dementia which particularly affects the short term memory, called the Wernicke-Korsakoff syndrome. Recently, however, evidence has been accumulating which indicates that alcohol is an important cause of dementia in an alarmingly high proportion of heavy drinkers. It emerges clearly from the evidence recently reviewed by Ron (1977) that if heavy drinking has gone on for a number of years, then damage to the brain as a whole and particularly to the frontal lobes of the brain will be found. The extent of the damage is related to the age of the drinker, to the length of time he has been drinking and to the amount of his drinking. It seems likely that this dementia will be an important factor militating against the successful rehabilitation of the longstanding alcoholic.

Possibly because it plays such an important part in the breakdown of alcohol, the liver is frequently damaged in alcoholics. As in the case of the brain, the degree of liver damage is in general related to the duration and extent of the drinking, but many individual patients fail to develop the anticipated degree of damage and the proportion of alcoholics who develop cirrhosis, the most severe type of damage, is in fact surprisingly small. Clearly for reasons as yet obscure, individual susceptibility is important.

The earliest type of damage is an infiltration of the liver with fat, this being an entirely reversible condition and seldom giving rise to any discomfort. The second stage of liver damage is alcoholic hepatitis, still a potentially reversible condition. In the severe case, there will be fever, loss of appetite, nausea, abdominal pain and jaundice. The most severe type of damage, cirrhosis, arises in only a small proportion of alcoholics. The damage is now irreversible, the functioning of the liver is likely to be severely impaired and the life expectancy is considerably shortened, although the outlook is vastly improved if drinking is completely discontinued.

The stomach is usually affected by chronic drinking and at least 30 per cent of alcoholics will suffer from chronic inflammatory stomach changes. This chronic gastritis causes nausea, vomiting and pain, particularly in the morning following a drinking bout. Functionally, it impairs the ability to absorb vitamins, amino acids and other essential nutrients from the diet.

The heart is also affected by alcohol. In a similar fashion to the liver, fatty infiltration of the muscle is an early effect. In a small proportion of people, the muscle cells are damaged so that their efficiency is impaired and the usual signs of heart failure, breathlessness on exertion, palpitations and swelling of the ankles eventually supervene. This alcoholic cardiomyopathy is a serious condition which calls for intensive treatment, coupled with total abstinence.

Alcohol is an important cause of anaemia, is associated with many different kinds of skin and eye conditions, plays an important part in pulmonary tuberculosis, chronic bronchitis and other chest diseases. There are in fact few organs or systems of the body which are not directly or indirectly affected by alcohol. Indeed, when one considers the harmful consequences of drinking, it becomes clear that the drug must have very attractive properties for mankind, otherwise it would surely not be taken.

3 DRINKING BEHAVIOUR

David Robinson

Introduction

Of all the substances which men have learnt to ingest, alcohol is
certainly among the most significant. Widespread in use and highly
valued as a ritual and social artefact, it has been tightly woven into
the fabric of everyday life. While no one can be certain, of course,
about which plant the primitive gatherers first cultivated, Keller (1976)
is confident that it was vitis, the grapevine, because: ' . . . as legend
tells us its fruit provided food that could be eaten both moist, (as
grapes) and dry (as raisins) and with little effort could be converted
into a drink of magical properties and potency: one that relieved
fatigue and assuaged pain, evoked gaiety, enhanced bravery, promoted
friendship and even facilitated communion with the invisible spirits
that seemed to control men's fate.'

While the chemical properties of alcohol provide a necessary base,
the behavioural concomitants of drinking depend as much on ideas of
what alcohol does to a person as they do on the physiological
processes that take place (Robinson, 1976). This chapter is not directly
concerned with alcoholism and alcoholics, but with alcohol and
drinking. It briefly discusses certain cultural variation and similarities
in drinking patterns, certain theories about the social role of alcohol,
and certain of the controls over alcohol consumption which operate
today.

Cultural Variations in Drinking Behaviour

Cultural practices in relation to alcohol range from eager drunkenness
to total abstinence. Anthropologists know this well, but those who
study the social problems associated with the use of alcohol do not
always take this fact into account. Even a brief mention of the varied
social patterns of drinking and the different functions which alcohol
plays in a society, emphasises the central importance of seeing the act
of drinking as part of a larger pattern of everyday social life. Alcohol is
a cultural artefact and the forms and meanings of drinking alcoholic
beverages are culturally defined. The form is usually quite explicitly
stipulated, including the kind of drink that can be used, the amount
and rate of intake, the time and place of drinking, the accompanying

23

ritual, the sex and age of the drinker, and the role behaviour proper to drinking. The meanings of drinking, its relation to other aspects of the culture and society, are usually more implicit. So drinking in a particular society or group may be either a sacred or a profane act, depending on the context.

At the extremes of the range of cultural practice the meanings are relatively clear. For example, among the Kofyar of Northern Nigeria, people make, drink, talk and think about beer. In the religious sphere, the Kofyar certainly believe that man's way to god is 'with beer in hand'. In contrast with those who consider alcohol to be essential and blessed are the people who regard it as destructive. The Hopi and other Pueblo Indian tribes of the American Southwest, for instance, felt that drinking so threatened their way of life that they successfully banned it from their settlements for many years.

The range of religious uses of alcohol is immense. Among the Aztecs, for example, worshippers at every major religious occasion had to drink to passing-out point, otherwise the gods would be displeased. In sharp contrast are those Protestant denominations which hold that alcohol is so repugnant spiritually that it is not allowed even symbolically in the communion rite. Yet another contrast is that provided in India, where a villager may pour an alcoholic libation in the worship of one type of deity, usually of the locality, while to do do to one of the deities of the classic pantheon would desecrate the temple and disgrace the worshipper.

Cultural expectations regulate the emotional consequences of drink. Drinking in one society may regularly release demonstrations of affection; in another it may set off aggressive hostility. Among Japanese, drinking is part of the fine ambience of pleasant physical sensation — when done at the proper time and place — and so is quite devoid of guilt or ambivalence. Conversely, there are other people among whom drinking is often accompanied by intense feelings of guilt.

The act of drinking can serve as a symbolic punctuation mark, differentiating one social context from another. The swift half pint in the pub before the commuter train leaves for suburbia helps separate the city and its work from the home and its relaxation. In more formal ritual, but with similar distinguishing intent, an orthodox Jew recites the Havdola blessing over wine and drinks the wine at the end of the Sabbath to mark the division between the sacred day and the rest of the week. Drinking may be quite purely symbolic, as it is in the Havdola rite and in the sacrament of communion, or it may be substantive as well as symbolic, as in the heavy drinking at Aztec religious ceremonies.

Among other symbolic uses of drinking are when one group or class within a larger society follows drinking patterns that serve as a badge marking them off from others. Such a badge may be deliberately adopted by the members of the group or may be ascribed to them by others, but when a sectarian group forbids drinking to its devotees, the prohibition is often deliberately taken as a counterbadge to separate the elect from the forlorn.

The physiological effects attributed to alcohol vary just as greatly among different peoples. Some are ready to feel high effect from a modicum of drink. Thus is has seemed to more than one Westerner that a Japanese man feels the convival glow almost before the first sip of saké can reach the stomach. Among Aleut Indians, drinking leads more to surly drunkenness than to mellow conviviality, but among them also a drinker becomes intoxicated after he has taken relatively small amounts of a fairly mild beverage. In other societies, a man must consume a large amount of alcohol before he shows that the drink has affected him. Similarly, the forms which hangovers and drunkenness take are heavily influenced by cultural interpretations (MacAndrew & Egerton, 1970).

A people who drink as heavily and as frequently as any group yet known, the Camba of eastern Bolivia, attribute no ill effects to their drinking, other than the irritations caused to the mouth and throat by their liquor, and undiluted distillate of sugar cane that contains 89 per cent ethyl alcohol. Most Camba men participate in recurrent drinking bouts, which may last for a whole weekend. A drinker may pass out several times in the course of a bout and, upon reviving, drink himself quickly into a stupor again. Dwight Heath, the anthropologist who has studied Camba drinking, observed that 'hangovers and hallucinations are unknown among these people, as is addiction to alcohol' (Heath, 1958). In general, addiction to alcohol seems to be quite rare outside certain societies of Western civilisation. Among most peoples whose men are expected to drink heavily and frequently, a man does not do any solitary drinking nor does he have withdrawal symptoms if he cannot get alcohol. He may not like to do without it, but he does not feel gripped by an iron compulsion to get a drink in order to be able to keep alive.

The behavioural consequences of drinking alcohol depend as much upon what people think that alcohol will do to them as on physiological processes. When a man raises his glass, it is not only the kind of drink that is in it, the amount he is likely to take, and the circumstances under which he will do the drinking that are specified in advance for him, but also whether the contents of the glass will cheer or stupefy, whether they will induce affection or aggression, guilt or unalloyed pleasure. These and many other cultural definitions attach to the drink even before it touches the lips.

Similarities in Drinking Behaviour across Cultures

Cultural variations in drinking practices are well documented, but there has been much less attempt to set out the similarities in the use of alcohol across cultures (Mandelbaum, 1965). One such regularity is that drinking is usually considered more suitable for men than for women. It is commonly a social rather than a solitary activity, and is done much more in the society of age mates and peers than with elders or in the family circle. Drinking together generally symbolises durable social solidarity — or at least amity — among those who 'share a drink'. This does not mean of course, that social drinking or 'sharing a drink' is necessarily a good thing. This assumption does, however, run through the alcoholism literature. *Social* drinking is good, goes the argument, but *solitary* drinking is bad. This assumption is based largely on the idea that social drinking is in a peer group which exercises appropriate social control regarding participants' drinking practices and behaviour.

Hayman (1967) pointed out the 'myth of social drinking':

> We cannot say that all who drink are alcoholics. But can we say that they are 'social drinkers' who, because of drinking, have hurt others by hostile criticism, made unwelcome passes at other men's wives, had unreasonable fights, given their children a model of drunkenness, squandered time needed for constructive pursuits, driven while in a drunken state, had accidents coming home from a cocktail party, impatiently punished their children, or sat detached from wife and children in front of the television set evening after evening in a semistuporous state, following several 'social' drinks before dinner? We need another category, 'antisocial drinking,' to replace much of what we call 'social drinking'.

Those who have studied alcoholism in work settings have found a kind of 'social contagion'. Foremen and supervisors who were heavy drinkers apparently reinforced heavy drinking among co-workers, encouraged some light drinkers to drink more frequently and in larger amounts than previously, and exerted pressure on non-drinkers to drink. In part, this was due to an environment conducive to frequent heavy drinking as expected behaviour conforming to group norms.

The viewpoint that solitary drinking is bad, in contrast with social drinking, seems based on several questionable assumptions. Solitary drinking is supposed to be 'hidden' and therefore not subject to social control and the social pressures of the peer group. The solitary drinker is often presumed to be a 'sicker' person than the social drinker both with respect to motivations for excessive drinking and to loss of control. The person who drinks by himself or herself is believed to be less likely to seek or obtain intervention from a support network or to come to the attention of resources for dealing with problem drinkers. Because women often face a greater stigma than men do from being drunk in public, it is often asserted that female problem drinkers are more likely than male problem drinkers to be solitary drinkers.

Rather than labelling 'social drinking' as desirable or good and 'solitary drinking' as undesirable or bad, the emphasis should be instead on the use the individual makes of alcohol, the consequences in terms of role functioning, physical and mental health, and on how the person copes with problems of living.

Drinking, throughout history, has usually been considered more appropriate for those who grapple with the external environment than for those whose task it is to carry on and maintain a society's internal activities. This distinction was anciently symbolised in India by the difference between the god Indra, the scourge of enemies, the thunderer, the roisterer, the heavy drinker, and Varuna, the sober guardian of order and morality. In ancient Greece, the worship of Dionysus could transport the worshipper into an extraordinary, even frenzied, state; that of Apollo encouraged only social morality. The Greeks successfully managed the two by assigning certain functions and occasions to the one deity and a different jurisdiction and festivals to the other. Drinking was a prominent feature of the Dionysiac rites but not at Apollonian ceremonies.

In general, warriors and shamans are more likely to use alcohol with cultural approval than are judges and priests. A priest is generally the conserver of tradition, the guide and exemplar for his fellows in precise replication of ritual in ways that please the gods. Drinking rarely goes with the priestly performance of ritual, except in symbolic usage, as in the Mass. But a shaman has personal relations with the supernatural, must directly encounter potent forces beyond ordinary society. Drinking is not often considered as interfering with this function.

When the fate of many hinges on the action of a single person, that person is usually not permitted to drink before performing the critical activity. The high priests of the Old Testament, beginning with Aaron, were particularly forbidden to drink 'wine nor strong drink' when discharging their priestly duties in the Sanctuary (Leviticus 10:9). Airline pilots today are generally forbidden to drink for a number of hours before flying as well as during the flight.

Yet another ban, that appears in various cultures, is imposed when it is considered dangerous to heighten the emotions of large numbers of people who gather at the same occasion. There is an inscription dating from about the year 5 BC near the stadium at Delphi which forbids the carrying of wine into the stadium on pain of a 5 drachma fine. There has been much discussion about banning alcohol from all soccer grounds and from Twickenham in an effort to curb hooliganism.

So, if we were to find a society in which women must drink more than men, in which drinking must be done alone or in the company of one's mentors and dependents, or in which the upholders of dogma, whether theological or political, are expected to drink more heavily than do others, we should know that we have encountered a society basically different from others so far reported upon.

The Social Role of Alcohol

Several anthropological studies have been concerned with broad questions about 'the place of alcohol in society' and hypothesised about a whole culture or even cultures. Horton (1943), for example, examined the files of the Cross-Cultural Survey in the Institute of Human Relates at Yale, extracted information on drinking for 77 different societies, constructed a scale of drinking behaviour based on the degree of insobriety commonly reached by adult male drinkers, and then related this to various indicators of 'subsistence anxiety'. The more primitive a society's food gathering techniques, the greater is the danger of food shortage and the more difficult are life conditions. These conditions, according to Horton, should create a relatively high amount of anxiety. Primitive subsistence techniques were, thus, assumed to be conducive to high anxiety levels and such societies also had a high level of insobriety.

All this, together with other supporting data, led Horton to conclude that 'the primary function of alcoholic beverages in *any* society is the reduction of anxiety'. Twenty years later Field (1962) re-examined Horton's theory, confirmed his finding that tribes with very primitive hunting and gathering economies tend to have more dunkenness than those with agricultural economies, but suggested that it is differences in the social organisation of the tribes which is responsible for the relation-

ship rather than subsistence anxiety: ' . . . drunkenness . . . is
determined less by the level of fear in a society than by an absence of
corporate kin groups with stability, permanence, formal structure, and
well defined functions.'

Other writers have developed classifications of various purposes or
'functions' on drinking. Bales (1959), for example, suggests that
alcoholic beverages can serve one or more of the following four
functions: religious, ceremonial, hedonistic, or utilitarian. Hedonistic or
pleasurable usages range from the conviviality engendered by drinking
with others to the euphoric feelings of getting high or having 'a glow
on', while utilitarian drinking, according to Bales, refers to the use of
alcohol to gain some 'relief or satisfaction of self-orientated, self-
centred needs'. More specifically alcohol's

> . . . everyday use to begin the day, to get rid of a 'hangover', to quiet
> hunger, to relieve stomach disorder, to get warm, to keep warm, to
> reward a child, to release sexual and aggressive tensions, to relieve
> emotional difficulties ranging from minor upsets and disappointments
> to deep grief, to restore consciousness in case of fainting and shock, to
> improve the physician's skill, to dispel fatigue and to promote sleep —
> all of these and more are utilitarian uses . . .

While writers such as Horton, Field and Bales attempt to provide
supra-cultural analyses of drinking behaviour, others — less ambitious —
have concentrated on the place of alcohol in one particular society or
one segment of society. However, in spite of the wealth of material on
clinical, moral and legal aspects of alcohol and associated problems,
there has been comparatively little basic descriptive work, particularly
on a national scale, on the central phenomenon — everyday drinking
habits. The most notable exception is the study by Cahalan, Cissin and
Crossley entitled *American Drinking Practices* (1969). In his introduction, Selden Bacon identifies the particular contribution of that
book:

> In the area of alcohol phenomena and alcohol-related problems there
> are studies and books and pamphlets, there are conferences and
> national organizations and films, there are newspaper reports and
> laws and handbooks on procedures, but they are often so disparate
> in language and purpose and target of attack that confusion, evasion
> and even outright hostility are all too frequent. One is concerned
> with disease, another with accidents, a third with sales control, a

fourth with criminal justice. One is based on biochemistry, another
on personality, a third on political art or science and a fourth on
community organization and public health. Cahalan, Cissin and
Crossley have centred attention on the phenomenon central to all
these approaches and central to all the problems no matter what
their form, no matter what discipline or language is employed:
namely, man using alcoholic beverages. Only as this phenomenon
occurs do any of the questions, any of the problems and any of the
controversies about cause or about policy for action even have
existence. Knowledge about this phenomenon is at the base. The
other knowledges, for example, law, psychiatry, metabolism, ethics,
may have much to offer this field, but they are not this field itself
and they developed their unique theories, methods and assumptions
in other settings. Man in society using alcoholic beverages and having
attitudes about that use, is the basis of this field. All too frequently
this essential and crucial pre-condition to all questions and answers,
has been forgotten.

Studies such as *American Drinking Practices* and similar surveys
which have been conducted recently in Scotland (Dight, 1976) and
south London (Cartwright *et al.*, 1975) are concerned with the who,
what, when, how much and why of drinking at a particular period
of time. They provide a broad back-cloth against which to set a
consideration of more specific questions such as why different religious,
age, sex, ethnic, social status, or other groups within a particular
society have different alcohol consumption patterns. For although
there have been very few national studies of everyday drinking
practices, there have been many studies of how specific segments of a
society define and use alcohol. For instance, a great deal of work
has been done, particularly in America, on the different drinking
patterns of major religious groups.

Three national drinking surveys, conducted since the Second World
War, found that among major religious groups Jews contained the
highest percentage of adult drinkers. A survey in 1947 put the figure at
87 per cent, one in 1963 put it at 90 per cent while Cahalan and Cissin
in 1968 put it at 92 per cent. By itself, of course, this information is of
no great interest. But juxtaposed with another body of material, which
suggests that Jews have the lowest rate of alcoholism among all major
religious groups, it raises a number of important questions. 'Why do the
highest consumers of alcohol have the lowest proportion of alcoholics?'
'Is there something about the way Jews use alcohol which prevents them

from becoming alcoholic?' 'Are Jews less likely to be defined as 'alcoholic' than other people with similar drinking habits and problems?' In short, how does one explain what Keller (1970) has called 'the great Jewish drink mystery'?

Bales, employing his fourfold classification of drinking 'functions', claims that alcoholism rates are low among Jews because of their 'ritual' attitude toward drinking. The frequent use of wine in religious ceremony leads the Jew to reject the use of drink for personal or hedonistic reasons. Hence, according to Bales, the idea of drinking to intoxication for some individual or selfish reason arouses such counter-anxiety that few Jews ever become alcoholics. Others have tried to relate Jewish sobriety to the need for Jews to conform to the best standards of society in order to avoid censure and blame, to the use of alcohol for 'instrumental' rather than 'affective' reasons and to Jewish values placed on education, self-control and rational behaviour.

These studies of Jewish drinking, and the studies of other segments of society, all aim to explain why some group drinks in a particular way. Along with all the other studies which were mentioned earlier, they attempt to place the use of alcohol in its cultural and social settings; to set out the relationship between alcohol consumption and other familial, religious, occupational, recreational and civic activities; and even, as in the case of writers such as Horton, Field and Bales, to speculate about the role of alcohol in human society as a whole. With a small number of notable exceptions, sociological research into these broad questions of a society's drinking and related practices is not very far advanced. But given the huge investments in time and money which are required to mount and successfully carry through such research this is, perhaps, hardly surprising. Nevertheless, an appreciation of the meaning which drinking has for members of the general population, and of the place it has in their everyday lives is increasingly being recognized as an essential part of any understanding of why particular people develop problems which are in some way connected with alcohol consumption.

Controls over Alcohol Consumption

It is not just broad cultural values or social norms which regulate the way in which alcohol is drunk. Drinking is not merely a matter of subtle inter-personal influences; it is regulated in the light of a whole series of other controls ranging from currency regulations and taxes to liquor licensing and laws about drunken driving.

A whole complex of controls, both direct and indirect, and varying between the major types of alcoholic beverage, can operate at all stages of importation, manufacture, distribution, sale and consumption. In Britain today, for example, it is permissible for anyone over five years old to consume intoxicating liquor except in the bar of licensed premises. On licensed premises, no one under 18 can purchase a drink. The only exception is for people over 16 who can buy beer, cider, porter or perry for consumption with a meal, provided that it is not served in a bar. It is an offence for anyone to buy drink for consumption in a bar by someone under 18. These distinctions between purchase and consumption mean that it is permissible, for example, for a 16 year old to take his 6 year old sister into a licensed restaurant and buy her as much beer, cider, porter or perry as she wanted with her meal. However, it would be an offence for the same 16 year old to buy his father half a pint of cider in the pub next door.

There are many other controls over consumption besides those of detailed liquor licensing. Taxes and duties, which are levied by national, and in some countries regional or city, authorities primarily for revenue purposes have a clear influence on the overall level of consumption. The possibility of taxation being used as much for control over consumption as a revenue-raising mechanism becomes more likely in those countries, like Britain, where the proportion of national revenue produced by alcohol taxes is gradually declining. Scandinavian countries are well ahead in the development of taxation policies with a built-in control of consumption element.

Control over advertising is another way in which governments attempt to control consumption together with, in some countries, laws governing marketing and profits. Behind all these broad societal controls is the knowledge that as overall availability is reduced so is overall consumption and so, as a result, is the level of alcohol-related problems. These issues will be discussed at greater length in Chapters 6 and 9.

Further indirect control is exercised through laws which deal with excessive consumption. These can be grouped into laws concerning drunkenness and those relating to drinking and driving. In Britain the drunkenness laws which are most frequently infringed and upheld by the courts at the present time concern 'simple drunkenness', 'being drunk and incapable', 'drunkennness with aggravations', and less frequently 'drunk in charge of a minor'. Convictions for drunkenness together with convictions for drunken driving produce a rate of approximately one alcohol-related offence for every two hundred adults in England and Wales.

Alcohol has not traditionally been considered as a target of international control, but the trend towards internationalisation and economic integration points to the need for international thinking in alcohol control policies. Some examples exist of efforts to transform international thinking into action. International Labour Organization Convention No. 95 on the protection of wages, for instance, contains provisions prohibiting the payment of wages in the form of beverages with a high alcohol content. Other examples are the ban on absinthe and the early international treaty attempting to control the alcohol trade in the former African colonies. However, for the most part, alcohol is carried freely over the borders without the controls that would be employed in the ordinary course of events if it were regarded as a drug whose consumption entails health risks.

In this chapter, I have tried to show how drinking and alcohol are closely bound up with everyday social life: rituals, ceremonies, relationships and rites. Since social behaviour differs widely from place to place, so everyday drinking practices differ just as widely. Nevertheless, in spite of the differences, there are also certain general similarities in drinking behaviour across cultures: men drinking more than women, drinking being a social rather than solitiary activity and one done in company with one's peers. Intimate social bonds and relationships are not, however, the only controls over an individual's consumption. The final part of the chapter drew attention to more formal controls over consumption, such as taxation, licensing laws, and laws concerning excessive consumption, all of which make control of alcohol availability a matter which, as Chapter 9 shows, governments can build into their broad preventive strategy.

4 LEARNING TO DRINK

Martin A. Plant

First Impressions

The great majority of adults in Britain drink alcohol at least
occasionally; alcohol consequently is part of the family environment
and is a 'social fact' for most young children. Social behaviour and
attitudes are learned by children from the important people in their
lives, who during the first few years of life are usually their parents or
those adults responsible for their upbringing. This process of learning
from adults is called *socialisation* which literally means being trained
to function as a member of society. Language, accent and
important aspects of behaviour are formed by imitating the important
adults in one's life. The influential people or 'significant others' in an
individual's life change as a person develops. At first most young
children spend almost all of their time with their parents but later
teachers play an important role and as children mature the peer group
of other young people of the same age becomes the main influence.
Social behaviour and attitudes change according to which particular
kinds of people are most significant at a given time.

Alcohol use is visible to most people from a very early age and
continues to be part of their social context as they grow older. People
learn about drinking in different ways, and may radically change both
their beliefs about alcohol and their mode of using it at different
stages in their lives. In this chapter, the basic psychological processes
of learning and reinforcement are briefly described and the development of a person's 'drinking career' is discussed in relation to social
pressures in Britain today.

Learning and Reinforcement

In discovering and relating to alcohol a person undergoes continuous
learning processes. People learn to associate the objects in their lives
with specific results. For example, a child may touch a flame once,
but is unlikely to repeat such an experiment. Psychologists describe
behaviour in relation to stimulus and response. One of the basic learning
theories is called Thorndike's Law of Effect, which states that if the
response to a stimulus (e.g. alcohol) is positive (pleasant), the behaviour
will be reinforced or strengthened. In other words, if people feel that
their drinking is beneficial they will continue to do it and if not they

will be less inclined to do so. Since success leads to repetition, people
are conditioned to alcohol by the reinforcement (consequences)
whether positive (relaxation, pleasure, praise, prestige) or negative
(hangover, headache, criticism). Over time, learning occurs when people
find drinking behaviour produces different reinforcements. At all times
the reinforcement derived from drinking is relative to reinforcements
derived from other sources. Many people become *habituated* by
experiencing the same thing over and over again; the effects wear off
and interest wanes. Possibly, this is why most excessive drinkers 'mature
out' of their heavy drinking.

As people move into different situations, they will learn to connect
specific stimuli (e.g. alcohol) with appropriate outcomes. They become
'conditioned' to react in relatively uniform ways to given cues (Walker,
1975). Most people manage to differentiate between different social
situations and to handle alcohol appropriately most of the time, but
problems arise if alcohol becomes a major preoccupation by providing
the only important positive reinforcements. Learning is an interaction
between the individual, his environment and specific stimuli within it.
In relation to drinking, alcohol is one of these stimuli. People continually change their ways of responding to it in different situations,
but are influenced both by their own personalities and life experiences
and by the expectations of their associates. Most alcohol use abides by
Thorndike's Law and is repeated only if beneficial. The difficulties
that sometimes result from alcohol use are largely due to the fact that
alcohol is a drug which may have negative long term reinforcement
(e.g. liver disease, physical dependence) which is not readily apparent
and which may be overshadowed by short term positive reinforcement
(e.g. having a good time). Also people are not wholly rational and what
may appear to be positive reinforcement may not be objectively
beneficial or positive for others.

Three important studies have been undertaken to examine what
children of different ages know about alcohol, and how they begin to
use it. While two of these were carried out in Scotland and one in
England, their results appear to be broadly applicable to the experiences
of children elsewhere in Britain (Jahoda & Cramond, 1972; Davies &
Stacey, 1972; Hawker, 1978).

The first of the two Scottish studies, both of which were carried out
in Glasgow, showed that most children begin learning about alcohol at
home and have formed definite impressions about it well before they
are old enough to attend primary school. Amongst a group of six year
olds, two-fifths were able to identify alcoholic drinks by smell and by

the age of ten this proportion had grown to three-fifths. The researchers found that many children taste alcohol when quite young (two-fifths of those aged six had tried it). Not only do young children very commonly see alcohol around so that they are able to recognise it; a majority of those in the Glasgow study were able to interpret drunken behaviour depicted in a film as the outcome of drinking. In addition, the evidence indicated that even before the age of six, most of the children had experienced encounters with drunken adults (Jahoda & Cramond, op. cit.).

An interesting finding of this study was that from the outset, boys were given more encouragement than were girls, to sample alcoholic drinks. The two sexes are reared in different ways and there are major differences between the later alcohol use by males and females. This issue has already been examined from a broad sociological perspective in Chapter 3.

Most young children have neutral or mildly favourable attitudes to alcohol but as they grow older they become more familiar with drinking at home and on special occasions may be given small amounts themselves. The Glasgow study showed that by the age of eight most children had attained a mastery of the concept of alcohol; they knew that alcoholic drinks were in a special category and associated these with undesirable adult behaviour which most had seen, often in their own home or in the streets. Between the ages of six and ten more children developed negative attitudes to alcohol and although most in this age group had no clear knowledge of the harmful effects of excessive drinking, they did have rather stereotyped ideas about drunks.

'An interpretation which fits the facts better is that children gradually learnt that alcohol is frowned upon by people in such institutions as schools and church. It would not be suprising if, in an authority setting like the school, they responded in terms of their awareness of the prevailing disapproval.' (Jahoda & Cramond, p.xiv.) Early attitudes to alcohol are generally formed at home but as the child spends more time outside the immediate circle of parents, these attitudes are modified by other adult authorities such as teachers, policemen and by the mass media.

Peer Pressure

The second Glasgow study by Davies and Stacey (1972) examined alcohol use amongst children aged 14-17. This study showed that as children grow up the influence of their home wanes and that of the teenage peer group becomes dominant and that by the age of 14, 92 per cent of boys and 85 per cent of girls in the study has tasted alcohol. Three years later only 2 per cent of boys and 4 per cent of girls in the study had not yet tried it. The negative and rather extreme attitudes of the pre-adolescent change dramatically by the time children pass puberty and teenagers form some very definite stereotypes of their own. The drinker is seen as sociable and tough, while the abstainer is not seen as socially desirable, but as weak and unsociable. Between the ages 10 and 14 the disapproving 'official' view of alcohol becomes reversed and most children have discarded this perspective for one positively reinforced by friends and associates of their own age amongst whom alcohol use is commonplace and encouraged.

Davies and Stacey found that with age, children began to consume more alcohol outside their own home and that such drinking in parks and streets was often carried out furtively with friends. Between the ages of 13 and 17 the peer group becomes firmly established as the influential reference point for drinking and young people begin to drink regularly because their friends do it, and because they regard drinking as socially desirable and prestigious. By the age of 17, Davies and Stacey found that most boys were drinking in pubs, while the majority of girls drink either in pubs or in dance halls. Possibly the adoption of secretive drinking, away from adult eyes, is attributable to the licensing laws which prohibit people under the age of 18 from buying alcohol in public bars. Possibly it is due to real or imagined parental disapproval.

There is little doubt that well before young men or women are legally old enough to drink in public bars, most will have been using alcohol for some time and will be deeply imprinted with attitudes supporting the view that alcohol is not simply another beverage like lemonade or coffee. Alcohol is widely regarded as a symbol of sociability, hospitality, maturity and enjoyment. By the time they are themselves approaching maturity, most adolescents begin to replace their earliest attitudes and behaviour with patterns they have learned to accept as adult. Drinking and, for many, smoking, are perceived as marks of maturity. They are things adults do and are adopted eagerly well before the age that the law allows.

A recent survey of 7,278 English schoolchildren aged 13-18 supported the Glasgow evidence that most children establish regular drinking habits in their early teens (Hawker, 1978). There is little doubt that for most teenagers the desired social norm is to be a light/moderate drinker. Davies and Stacey found that such approval is not extended to heavy drinking, which is perceived as excessive and as unsociable.

Imitative Drinking

Most young people are brought up in homes where alcohol is used in moderation, without causing serious or recurrent problems. A minority is not; some children have parents who drink excessively and who suffer serious consequences because of this and others are brought up in homes where alcohol is not consumed and have parents who are hostile to drinking. Neither group of parents is able to provide a model of moderate drinking which, if copied, would not be likely to create problems. There is evidence that many people who later in life experience difficulties with their drinking come from homes where their parents either abused alcohol or were rigid abstainers. A study of children in English and Irish families concluded that the latter were frequently discouraged from drinking, while the former were not. Subsequently, the Irish children were more likely than the English to suffer harmful consequences due to drinking, even if their alcohol consumption was low (O'Connor, 1978).

Many young people reproduce the drinking behaviour of their parents (Hawker, 1978) and thus often copy their moderate, harmless, patterns of drinking. Like O'Connor, Davies and Stacey found that the children of parents with prohibitive views on drinking were sometimes likely to drink more than those whose parents were permissive. Hawker found 'that although the parents who disapproved of drinking were in the minority, their influence over their children's drinking behaviour was greater than that of other parents. The proportion of non-drinkers and occasional drinkers for both sexes was considerably higher than the corresponding proportion for children whose parents approved of their drinking.'

Davies and Stacey reported that youthful heavy drinkers were particularly likely to be hostile to the older generation and to authority figures such as parents and teachers and that in addition, heavy drinkers scored high on the psychological trait of 'trouble/precocity', which is a good indicator of delinquent behaviour. Drinking (amongst other things) may be chosen by rebellious young people as a means of asserting their individuality and maturity. It is possible that the more parents discourage drinking and emphasise that it is undesirable, the greater the seductions of peer group encouragement to drink will be.

Adult Drinking Careers

Drinking behaviour, as outlined in the previous chapter, varies with social class, sex and with national traditions and customs; therefore to a large extent the style of drinking a person adopts will reflect the learning processes involved in face-to-face contacts with other people. An individual tends to drink the same kinds of beverage and in a similar manner to his/her associates at any given time. A person will usually adopt his/her style of drinking to suit given social circumstances. There is evidence that most adults pass through a fairly clearcut 'drinking career' once they have begun to drink regularly (Edwards *et al.*, 1972; Dight, 1976; Plant & Pirie).

Drinking is positively reinforced by many social and psychological pressures. Some advertising has in the past been specifically directed at young people, and has reinforced the belief that drinking is a symbol of being sexually attractive and successful, of being masculine, or feminine, of being mature, and of 'the good life' in general. Without exception, British surveys of drinking behaviour have shown that the section of the community who are the heaviest drinkers are young, unmarried people (mainly males) who are in their late teens and early twenties and that older people generally drink much less. The survey of Scottish drinking habits by Susan Dight (1976) found that 30 per cent of the alcohol con-sumed by the sample was drunk by a mere 3 per cent of those inter-viewed and that this small minority was young, single, working-class males. There are several reasons why young people are the heaviest drinking group in the community. One reason is their great spending power while still single and free from family commitments, since income is probably an important influence on a young person's alcohol consump-tion. Hawker's investigation of English schoolchildren disclosed that 'the most important influence discouraging young people to drink was an increase in the price of alcohol which was given by a larger propor-tion of both sexes of frequent drinkers compared with non-drinkers and infrequent drinkers.'

Perhaps of more importance than financial freedom on leaving school is the lifestyle of many single young people in which drinking is widely regarded as a sociable thing to do and many, if not most, social activities outside the home revolve around, or at least involve, the con-sumption of alcohol. Drinking is increasingly used as a catalyst to relax-ation and enjoyment. Some individuals use alcohol to produce 'Dutch courage' to conceal their sexual or social lack of confidence, while others drift into temporary periods of relatively heavy drinking due to their social group. Drinking is highly correlated with cigarette smoking and some young people also use illegal drugs such as cannabis and LSD. It is not surprising that these are generally quite heavy drinkers and cigarette smokers. The majority of young people do not use alcohol in excess, and reduce their consumption dramatically once they get married and settle down.

Drinking usually occurs as part of some more general social activity, which is almost always shared. Although some young people drink excessively and get into trouble due to drinking, few become physically dependent upon or 'addicted' to alcohol since this generally takes quite a few years of heavy drinking to develop. The majority of difficulties young drinkers get into are due to high alcohol consumption over a short period of time leading to drunkenness; thus many young people get into fights, or have accidents while drunk but most do not and individual drinking behaviour is very highly correlated with social class and with sex. Women drink far less than men, and get into trouble with drinking less often (though this is changing rapidly). Middle-class people are far less likely to get into fights while drunk. The majority of young people who get deeply involved with drinking are young men from socially deprived backgrounds who generally have a multiplicity of social and psychological problems. Such individuals have little stake in the conventional workaday world and adopt the lifestyle of the 'pub regular' or heavy drinker in response to their many problems (Plant, 1975).

Fortunately, the majority of these youthful alcohol abusers mature out of their heavy drinking as they find jobs or other interests, and particularly when they marry (Cahalan, Cissin & Crossley, 1969). In most cases alcohol consumption is reduced before dependence is created, or before serious or irreversible physical damage occurs. The majority of people continue to use alcohol in moderation and suffer no ill effects because of this; for most people alcohol is simply an aid to enjoyment, and a facet of social activities. Long-term problems arise if drinking and the social situations connected with it are adopted as the main interest and reference point. Young people who begin to drink heavily reduce their consumption once they form relationships which lead them away from their heavy drinking peer group. Thus, they may drink a lot while at college or university, then drink far less when working as teachers or accountants. People drift into and out of different stages of drinking at different times (Matza, 1969). Some people who get into trouble through drinking are scared off by their first bad experience and moderate their consumption thereafter. In general, a person will drink only to the extent that it is regarded as rewarding and pleasant in relation to all of the other alternative activities. So long as a person is able to enjoy things such as work or marriage, alcohol will probably be used in moderation. Drinking is generally a social activity which is limited by the availability of other social activities and other sources of pleasure.

When a person drinks heavily, it is usually for purely social reasons and his drinking habits may be influenced by the type of job he or she has and some occupational groups have far greater alcoholism rates than others. These include the drink trade, seamen, servicemen, journalists and doctors. The 'high risk' of such occupations is probably due to factors such as available of alcohol during working hours, to strong pressure to drink from workmates, to separation from a normal home life or to freedom from supervision (Plant, 1977). This is discussed at greater length in Chapter 7. A person may drink heavily if in a social group where this is the norm and then drink less if in a different social group. The majority of heavy drinkers are essentially social animals and spend much of their time with other heavy drinkers. Most public bars have their little group of 'regulars', people who use drinking as their main social activity. To such people drinking is part of their lifestyle, from which they derive considerable social support and status. If, eventually, a person's drinking causes serious problems, that may warrant a reappraisal of the situation. In any event, a person is likely to continue with his/her given way of drinking until a more attractive alternative becomes available. In most cases, people who get into difficulties with their drinking have to change their way of life not only by modifying their former patterns of alcohol use, but by attaching themselves to new social groups and by finding new interests and beliefs. One of the reasons why Alcoholics Anonymous helps some problem drinkers to abstain is that it offers both a new set of beliefs and a supportive group of associates. In many cases, people simply drift into harmful excessive drinking for social reasons; not all turn to the bottle because of an upsetting life event.

Alcohol is not only used for social reasons. It is a depressant drug and does produce an altered state of consciousness so that some people drink excessively almost as a form of self-medication because they wish to dim their awareness, to relax, to seek oblivion.

To conclude, throughout their lives people learn different things about alcohol. What these things are will depend upon their social group and social background at any given time. Because socialisation or learning how to behave in society is a continuing process, drinking behaviour generally changes with different social pressures. Problems are often only temporary, since people are frequently able to learn new ways of using or of avoiding alcohol.

5 DEFINING ALCOHOLISM

D.L. Davies

What we do about a problem is determined very largely on how we view that problem. For that reason, if for no other, it would be as well to decide in what way alcoholism is to be defined. Unless there is agreement on this, statistical data of any value are unlikely to be gathered, there will be no sure basis on which to determine the extent of the problem at any one time, and even less on which to decide whether it is increasing. Without such information there can be no likelihood of planning future provision for dealing with the problem.

Why there should be so many ways of viewing alcoholism is an interesting question. No doubt the various elements in this piece of human behaviour, the social, moral, ethical, religious and legal implications, make any simple definition difficult to arrive at, whilst the likely consequences of any one view lead often to counter-measures — prohibition, for example — which are both repugnant to the majority and provedly ineffective, and in conflict with conclusions to be derived from another view.

For these and other reasons, the World Health Organisation in 1951 set up an Expert Committee to look at the matter in its own right, and its first report (WHO, 1952) defined alcoholism as: 'any form of drinking which in its extent goes beyond the traditional and customary "dietary" use, or the ordinary compliance with the social drinking customs of the whole community concerned, irrespective of the aetiological factors leading to such behaviour and irrespective also of the extent to which such aetiological factors are dependent upon heredity, constitution, or acquired physiopathological and metabolic influences.' This statement takes up deviance as the criterion, deviance from the 'normal' quantity of intake of the whole community by way of excess, or deviance of what one might call motivation to drink. Very wisely, it avoided any attempt to involve causation as an element in definition.

The Expert Committee met again within a year, and had second thoughts, expressed in the definition of August, 1952, which is the one most widely quoted ever since. This ran: 'Alcoholics are those excessive drinkers whose dependence upon alcohol has attained such a degree that it shows a noticeable mental disturbance or an interference with their bodily and mental health, their interpersonal relationships and their smooth social and economic functioning, or who show the pro-dromal signs of such developments. They therefore require treatment.'

Some omissions of the earlier definitions are rectified. What would seem to most people to be obvious elements in any definition, matters of harm resulting from drinking, or the propensity to carry on drinking when there would seem to be good reason to desist, now appear. The earlier statement equates with the excessive drinking referred to here, whilst the propensity to drink is taken care of in the word 'dependence', and harm is itemised to cover mental, physical and social aspects of life, in the broadest sense of these terms.

The word 'prodromal' is of ominous significance. It is used in medical parlance to indicate early signs or symptoms, to be followed later by others (e.g. a faint rash, before the full-blown rash, fever and malaise of, say, measles). If one is at this point uncertain as to how the Expert Committee viewed alcoholism, the matter is placed beyond all doubt in the last sentence, since to require treatment is synonymous with being ill.

One cannot be sure what the term 'dependence' used here really means. Its present meaning was set out by the World Health Organisation some 12 years later, when they proposed that it should replace the word addiction, earlier in current use (a matter to be mentioned later). The present meaning of the term dependence, they set out at some length as follows (WHO, 1964): 'A state, psychic and sometimes also physical, resulting from the interaction between a living organism and a drug, characterised by behavioural and other responses that always include a compulsion to take the drug on a continuous or periodic basis in order to experience its psychic effects, and sometimes avoid the dis-comfort of its absence. Tolerance may or may not be present. A person may be dependent on more than one drug.'

In simple language, dependence is seen from this to mean a need to go on taking a drug to avoid either feelings of discomfort (psychological dependence) or actual physical symptoms, such as trembling (physical dependence). In the case of some drugs, either psychological or physical dependence usually results, but with other drugs it seems to be a matter of degree which determines the precise form of the withdrawal state at any particular time.

If we attach the current meaning of dependence to the same term used in 1952, then dependence as now understood is not synonymous with alcoholism in the WHO definition. Only when dependence goes on to result in harm, it would seem, does alcoholism begin.

It is because of these two key elements in that definition that it has become unacceptable to a great many people.

It is common enough for a man to drink regularly, perhaps daily, over perhaps 20 years, with nothing to suggest that he is in any way harming himself or others, until one day he experiences memory loss or some physical complaint, which is clearly the consequence of his earlier drinking. Did he become an alcoholic on that day or was he not dependent for some years before that incident? Is he no longer an alcoholic when the incident has been resolved and he no longer suffers in that way, even though his propensity to drink as before remains unchanged?

The second element in that definition, the implication of illness, is equally unacceptable to many. By including it in the definition, it precludes enquiry as to whether the behaviour of alcoholics justifies that conclusion. One valuable aspect of a definition of alcoholism is that it enables us to answer by scientific enquiry the question of whether or not it is an illness. It also enables us to answer other questions of importance, such as the inevitability of return, once the behaviour has ceased, or what goals should determine the sort of help we may be able to offer to alcoholics.

The term 'disease' is, if anything, more difficult to define than alcoholism, especially when it is so widely used in senses for which it was never intended. Wife beating, baby battering, football hooliganism, making money (or losing it), and many other aspects of human behaviour are now described as diseases; society's 'ailments' are 'diagnosed', and expressed in terms of 'social pathology'.

The chief reason for dragging the idea of disease into the WHO definition was no doubt the popular misconception (which still persists) that Jellinek had lent the weight of his authority to it, though the thinking behind it goes back to 1804 at least, when Thomas Trotter wrote: 'This disease, I mean the habit of drunkenness, is like some other mental derangements . . . ' (Trotter, 1804)

Some alcoholics, from the 1930s onwards, understandably found this idea attractive, suggesting, as it seems, that they were not responsible for their condition. The illness concept carries no such universal implications, of course. A venereologist, who acquires gonorrhoea from intercourse with a known prostitute, would look very foolish if he were to disclaim responsibility for his illness.

Of course, the kind of disease which those alcoholics who support the disease concept have in mind is something which would describe a condition preceding their drinking, something constitutional, that is to say, present from their earliest days, and therefore likely to be in the nature of a biochemical or psychological abnormality. It was Jellinek

(1960) who reviewed all the evidence on those counts and found none to justify the view that alcoholics were so tainted before their alcoholic behaviour became evident. It was also Jellinek who stated the view, held before his time by some and more recently by a fast growing majority, that many alcoholics (some would say most) become so simply by drinking in accordance with the social customs of the hard drinking group to which they belong. At some point, he said, whatever the genesis of excessive drinking, 'alcohol progressively takes over until it becomes the decisive factor in what the addict may or may not do'.

How then is it that Jellinek has become misunderstood? He was pressed into writing about the 'disease concept' of alcoholism, and agreed against his better judgement, after vainly proposing that instead he should be allowed to write about 'the disease conception' of alcoholism. Presumably under the latter title, he could have postulated that *some* alcoholics are constitutionally different from ordinary people, examined the available evidence for that, and drawn the best conclusion, without throwing doubt on the cause of alcoholism in the majority of alcoholics.

He was well aware of the danger in allowing himself to be pushed into writing what he was asked and expressed this very clearly in a statement in 1952:

> The lay public uses the term alcoholism as a designation for any form of excessive drinking, instead of as a label for a limited and well-defined area of excessive drinking behaviour. Automatically, the disease conception of alcoholism becomes extended to all excessive drinking, irrespective of whether or not there is any physical or psychological pathology involved in the drinking behaviour. Such an unwarranted extension of the disease conception can only be harmful because, sooner or later, the misapplication will reflect on the legitimate use too and, more importantly, will tend to weaken the ethical basis of social sanctions against drunkenness.

Very few have heeded that warning. It is still commonly asserted that 'alcoholism is a disease', quoting Jellinek as the authority for it, and without stating what kind of disease, what is the evidence, or indeed, if making the statement helps us in any way to determine what should be done with those who are said to exhibit the disease.

The most Jellinek felt able to say was that those drinkers who seemed to go on drinking once they had started a drinking occasion (the so-called loss of control drinkers) were the sub-group with the postulated constitutional abnormality. Only two comments are needed here. The propensity to behave in this way is very well explained by modern learning theory, and capable of being induced in healthy animals, and equally evident in people who become dependent on other drugs (barbiturates, nicotine, morphine, heroin and other substances), where there is no question of previous constitutional abnormality. Further, Jellinek himself admitted that there was little or no evidence *even in the groups defined* to show constitutional predisposition, but leaned to the view that, nevertheless, there *must* be such.

This most surprising conclusion to the long, careful, objective evaluation of the evidence, which all pointed the other way, can only be explained in the light of Jellinek's views about human behaviour in general. Like other psychoanalysts of his day, all human behaviour was to him explicable in terms of psychoanalytic theory. If slips of the tongue, lapses of memory and other features of everyday life have a psychopathology, then drinking behaviour could hardly be an exception. The man who had preceded Freud to the rostrum at the second International Psychoanalytic Congress at the age of 20, who had been analysed by Ferenczi at the age of 26, who regarded psychoanalysis 'not just as a psychiatric technique but as a distinct science of mental disorders . . . probably the only science in this field which is properly rounded out and conceptualised', the man who had made it clear as chairman of the research committee into schizophrenia at the Worcester State Hospital (before starting his new life in the study of alcoholism), that 'we urgently recommend hiring a competent psychoanalyst. We are not favourable to psychoanalysis by "educated readers"', in short, E.M. Jellinek, when faced with the question of whether or not this striking behaviour in the alcoholic did or did not have a psychic determinant, could not possibly have answered in other terms than he did.

No doubt the general dissatisfaction with the WHO definition, particularly its weakness on the aspect of dependence, and its unnecessary introduction of the debatable disease origin of alcoholism, had something to do with the recent publication from WHO entitled *Alcohol Related Disabilities* (Edwards *et al.*, 1977).

Alcohol Dependence Syndrome

This syndrome is not easy to summarise, and all who are interested are urged to read the document themselves (Edwards, *et al.*, 1977). Instead of drawing a line between dependence and harm, it would seem to draw a line between normal and abnormal, putting into the first bracket what we would otherwise have called psychological dependence and into the second physical dependence. The thinking behind this seems to be that dependence on drugs has very much in common with dependence on other substances and practices, which are not 'inevitable abnormalities', whilst 'physiological dependence, as evidenced by substance-specific disturbance on drug withdrawal, on the other hand, is an abnormal condition (Edwards & Grant, 1977). This concept seeks to distinguish between dependence, which may be harmless, and disability, which it defines as impairment in physical, mental or social functioning. However, elsewhere in the same document, it is stated that 'dependence predicates the existence of profound and central disability' whilst under alcohol disability is included the alcohol dependence syndrome itself.

'Dependent disability' implies the probability, it goes on to say — 'of a continued or intermittent pattern of drinking behaviour, such that over time a considerable summated experience of alcohol-related disabilities will accrue.' It is mentioned as existing after an attack of the alcohol withdrawal syndrome, and so long as he is liable to relapse into that syndrome, a man is 'disabled by reason of the dependency itself'.

Clearly, this is an unfamiliar language, which would, however, merit mastery if the practical gains were evident. The applications are cited in some detail in the publication referred to and it is for consideration whether rephrasing the questions posed by alcoholism in the fields of prevention, treatment, research and so on, in this language, opens up better prospects of making headway than hitherto.

The syndrome is described by Edwards (Edwards & Grant, 1977) as provisional and there has been little time as yet to see how it fares, but caution should be advised in using the new terminology before it has been understood and mastered.

Drug Addiction

Alcohol is a drug, like many others, which induces dependence when used in certain minimal quantities and with a certain frequency of ingestion.

It is surprising, to say the least, that WHO set up its Expert Committee to define alcoholism, as already described, when there was current at that time a generally accepted definition of drug addiction, which ran as follows:

Drug addiction is a state of periodic or chronic intoxication, detrimental to the individual and to society, produced by repeated consumption of a drug (natural or synthetic). Its characteristics include:

(i)   an overpowering desire or need (compulsion) to continue taking the drug and to obtain it by any means;

(ii) a tendency to increase the dose;

(iii) a psychic (psychological) and sometimes a physical depen-dependence on the effects of the drug.

The first sentence of this is of great importance. It clearly states what is omitted or obscure in the definitions we have discussed so far, namely that the definition is *not* to concern itself with the effects of drugs on single occasions. Such effects are called acute effects, and are quite different from the effects of repeated, long-term usage. Acute effects may be harmful, causing death on occasions, and relatively high quantities of drug intake are needed to bring out this harmful aspect. Chronic effects may show little or no apparent impact on the individual on repeated occasions in the long series of ingestions, and the doses may be modest, but in this way dependence develops.

Where the drug addiction definition proved weak, for all such drugs and not just for alcohol, was in its failure to separate dependence from harm. We know now that long-term harm hinges on critical quantities and frequency of ingestion, and theoretically, at all events, might be severe while dependency is only mild. It may also be artificial, in that it is punishable because in breach of the law, but not otherwise detrimental to the wellbeing of the individual or society. The definition failed in trying to itemise too closely the features listed (i) to (ii), because there is great variability between drugs on these counts.

Thus, the man who is unbearable to live with for weeks whilst abstaining from smoking (thereby displaying his dependence), is *not* overwhelmed — see (i). In the case of cocaine, there is no tendency to increase the dose — see (ii). Amphetamine causes only psychological dependence (which can be very severe indeed).

What the definition did not cover was long term harmless depend-ence, with no tendency to increase the dose — very common with opium and barbiturates — which the Brain Committee (Brain, 1961) referred to as 'stabilised addiction', meaning a harmless variant of a harmful state.

It was this increasing confusion which led WHO to drop the term 'addiction' for 'dependence', which it subsequently defined as has been described above.

Had there been no WHO Expert Committee in 1951, had alcoholism been regarded as alcohol addiction within the contemporary definition, it would have stuck out from the general definition as no more of a sore thumb than any other drug addiction, and in the course of time we would have arrived at the concept of alcoholism as two things, (a) dependence and (b) long term harm, as we have with the other drugs in this category.

Jellinek's Definition

Oddly enough, Jellinek said that we might have to define alcoholism as any use of alcoholic beverage that caused any damage to the individual, to society or to both. If, to avoid the nonsensicality of regarding a youth who breaks his leg when tipsy after his first introduction to alcohol as an alcoholic (which Jellinek's definition would allow), we marry Jellinek's concept to that of the old definition of drug addiction (which clearly precluded acute effects), then we arrive at a suggested definition as follows: 'Alcoholism is the intermittent or continual ingestion of alcohol, leading to dependence or harm.'

What difficulties does such a definition entail? Provided that we are prepared to suspend judgement on the validity of a number of myths arising from the muddled thinking of the past, probably none.

If a man is merely dependent on alcohol, and so alcoholic under this definition, there is no need for him to cut down or stop drinking, unless there is good reason to believe, by looking closely at him, that he is building up trouble for himself in the future. More positively, this definition, more than any other, focuses attention on prevention as a hopeful way of dealing with alcoholism.

Again, on the positive side, by including dependence as one criterion of alcoholism, in a particular case, attention is directed to what we all know but tend to forget, that treating alcoholics is largely treating their dependence, whereas treatment of the harm is relatively straightforward and requires a matter of days or weeks, rather than months or years.

What are we to understand by all the other terms used in this field: heavy drinker, social drinker, heavy social drinker, problem drinker, relief drinker, weekend drinker, fiesta drinker, Stammtisch—Trinker, and many others? The answer is simple: avoid using them, unless you feel able to define them in any helpful way. Many are merely descriptions of patterns of drinking, and problem drinker is merely a euphemism for alcoholic, since, if he has, or has generated for others, a problem arising from his intermittent or continual drinking, then he is an alcoholic.

Symptomatic Drinking

The most serious objection is that from time to time we encounter people who have become alcoholic, in the sense defined, without much of a leading-in period of exposure to alcoholic beverages. This is best seen in mania, schizophrenia, dementia, or severe personality disorder. Where these states are reversible, e.g. in mania, the harmful drinking stops as suddenly as it began. This is, in fact, a small but distinct variety of alcoholism, best termed symptomatic alcoholism, the recognition of which is a psychiatric matter.

The last objection is that by separating the harm of acute from that of chronic intoxication, we are drawing an artificial distinction. It is true that drunkenness may mark both, because the man who repeatedly gets drunk may well be on the way to dependence and long-term harm (alcoholism), whilst the alcoholic is likely to drink more frequently than the non-alcoholic, and so be more vulnerable to repeated drunkenness.

The answer is that, if we begin by not defining alcoholism as proposed, and just look at all drinking behaviour, which entails harm, we finish up with two broad categories of drinkers, those who are young, mass their intake of drink on certain nights of the week, and produce harmful effects of a dramatic kind (e.g. violence), and older people, whose drinking is more spread out over the week, and who produce harm of a less dramatic kind (alcoholic diseases of the body or mind in the main).

Reflection suggests that society's response to these types of harm originates very differently. In the former case, it concerns police control, traffic regulations, the desirability of not compressing licensing hours too closely to avoid pressure to drink, whilst the response to the other kind of harm is more medically based, along with long-term social work involvement.

This may be the place to note that, if we try to use measures of harm to gather statistics about alcoholism (see Chapter 6), some, like drunkenness, will span acute and chronic effects; some, like cirrhosis of the liver, will be chronic effects, where there is little room for the influence of individual attitudes (say, of certifying doctors), whilst some measures, such as admission to hospital for alcoholic disorders, may depend most on availability of beds and admission policies, so that considerable variation may occur at different times and places.

The discussion outlined here has aimed at clarifying our thoughts about what it is which we are dealing with when we encounter someone who, for one reason or another, has an involvement with alcohol, which is actually or potentially harmful. Only if we are clear in our own minds about this hypothetical person, can we begin to offer help along rational lines or devise preventive programmes which will command the respect of those whose duty it is to provide such.

Whether or not this aim has been achieved remains to be seen, but the effort is necessary, for we cannot remain content with the summary of the position set out by Wexberg (1951), when he wrote, 'In no other area of research and social or medical endeavour have slogans so extensively replaced theoretical insights as a basis for therapeutic action as in alcoholism.'

6 EPIDEMIOLOGY

S.J. Shaw

Epidemiology is the study of the distribution of diseases and of the factors which influence this distribution. Epidemiologists usually describe the distribution of diseases either in terms of 'incidence' – the number of new cases occuring over a specific period, or in terms of 'prevalence' – the total number of cases at a specific moment or over a specific period. Epidemiologists have reported, for example, that the *prevalence* rate of alcoholism used to be five or six times higher amongst men than amongst women, but is now only two or three times as high, because the *incidence* or alcoholism amongst women has increased rapidly over the last decade.

Although such a pronounced change may seem fairly clear cut, rates of incidence and prevalence should never be accepted just at their face value. If the figures above, for example, refer only to hospital admissions for alcoholism, then we cannot be certain that there are now more women with drinking problems than there were previously. The explanation might be rather that women are now more open about their drinking problems and more likely to seek help. Alternatively, it could be that psychiatrists have become more likely to diagnose women as alcoholics because of publicity about the subject, or simply because there has been an increase in the number of alcoholism treatment settings into which women can be admitted. This possible influence of changing diagnostic fashion upon rates of incidence and prevalence is a complication endemic not just to the epidemiology of alcoholism but to psychiatric epidemiology in general, whereas in more traditional epidemiological areas there are fewer such problems of validity. Indeed, some rates of incidence and prevalence, such as those of physical diseases with very definite symptoms, can be established with near certainty by epidemiological research. The more loosely defined the condition, however, the more uncertainty arises over the reliability and validity of epidemiological evidence, and since it has been remarked that 'no problem of definition in medicine is more baffling than that of defining mental illness' (MacMahon, 1967) it is not surprising that the epidemiology of mental illness is bedevilled by inconsistencies and contradictions. The difficulties persist whatever the type of measurement used. If the epidemiologist uses the numbers of persons diagnosed as suffering some particular mental illness, then he must bear in mind that the procedures for diagnosing this condition might vary from doctor to doctor. On the other hand, the epidemiologist cannot rely just on data from surveys of the general population, because there are no systematic case finding techniques which are used consistently in surveys to detect persons with a particular mental health problem, and hence to establish rates of incidence and prevalence.

It is only to be expected then that these difficulties which afflict the whole of psychiatric epidemiology should be borne out within the epidemiology of drinking problems. Indeed, there is even some debate about whether the term 'epidemiology' should be applied here at all, since many experts have argued that it is inappropriate or incorrect to consider alcoholism to be a disease, and have questioned whether there is one set of behaviour and experiences related to alcohol which can meaningfully be placed under the umbrella of one inclusive term such as 'alcoholism' or 'problem drinking'. Alcohologists have tried without success for many years to construct a universally acceptable definition of alcoholism (see Chapter 5) which may suggest that there is no such definition to be found and that alcohol problems are not amenable to any simple classification. Epidemiologists nevertheless have been expected to express their results in terms of the number of alcoholics or problem drinkers, and the tendency to use terms and categorisations about which there has been no general agreement has created inevitable inconsistencies and ambiguities. As the World Health Organisation noted in 1977, 'The extent of problems related to alcohol consumption is difficult to gauge, partly because assessments are often hinged on the term "alcoholism" whose definition varies widely.' (Edwards *et al.*, 1977.) It is in effect impossible to state exactly how many alcoholics there are, simply because alcohologists have found it impossible to agree on exactly what constitutes an alcoholic.

Whatever the rights and wrongs of their arguments, and whatever the merits and demerits of particular definitions and categorisations, the implication for the validity of epidemiological data is quite clear — namely that one should treat with considerable caution any epidemiological statistics which purport to be precise prevalence rates of alcoholism. Such specific figures can only be produced by glossing over the real difficulties in measurement. In the case of arbitrarily defined conditions like alcoholism, the estimated prevalence rate will simply depend on the working definition which the epidemiologist decides to use. This was amply illustrated in a general population survey of San Francisco conducted by Clark (1966), who demonstrated how different definitions of alcoholism created all sorts of prevalence rates. A very strict definition of alcoholism produced a rate of three per thousand, but using a variety of indices made the prevalence estimates increase to 62 per thousand adults. If all criteria were employed, including any indications of drinking problems past or present, moderate or severe, then the prevalence reached an extraordinary 272 per thousand. Which rate is the most appropriate measure? A low rate might reflect a limited view of the problem; a higher rate might be an exaggeration. The basic difficulty is that there is no distinct point at which alcohol 'use' ends and alcohol 'abuse' begins. The only certainty is that the wider the defining criteria of the problem, the more cases will fit the definition.

The Two Worlds of Alcohol Problems

The difficulties over definition make it quite difficult to gain a reasonable perspective of the size of the problem. In 1975, for instance, the Department of Health and Social Security concluded that 'different surveys indicate that about 400,000 persons in England and Wales (about 11 in every 1,000 of the adult population) have a serious drink problem' (DHSS, 1975). In the same year, less than 15,000 persons were admitted into mental hospitals in England and Wales with a primary or secondary diagnosis of alcoholism or alcoholic psychosis. The same discrepancy has been replicated in studies of individual Health Districts. A 1974 study of a representative sample of the general population of a Health District in South London determined the proportion of the population who were 'excessive drinkers' to be 2.1 per cent and the prevalence rate of 'people with problems from drinking' to be 3.5 per cent. However, in the same year, only 0.16 per cent of residents of the District received psychiatric treatment for alcoholism (Cartwright *et al.*, 1975). A similar discrepancy was found by Edwards *et al.* (1973) who identified 3.13 per cent of a general population sample as having a drinking problem, compared to only 0.47 per cent who had been recognised as alcoholics by one or more of a number of agencies in the same area, such as courts, clergy, employers and doctors. As Davies (1974) has remarked, 'One of the unsolved mysteries of alcoholism has been the report from surveys carried out by general practitioners of how few alcoholics they see, and the generally accepted findings of epidemiologists who stress how many there are.'

Room (1977) referred to these two types of estimates as the 'two worlds of alcohol problems' — the relatively small number of heavily damaged drinkers who exhibit symptoms traditionally associated with the concept of alcoholism, and the wider range of people who seem to experience different types and degrees of problems due to their drinking. In his own survey, Room found that a substantial proportion of American men moved in and out of this 'problem drinking population' within a three-year period (Cahalan & Room, 1974).

In part, the discrepancy noted by Davies and Room reflects the fact that surveys produce prevalence rates whilst hospital admissions are incidence rates. But the major reason why the figures do not tally is that different criteria are being employed. General population surveys usually determine whether respondents are 'alcoholics' or not by asking them if they have experienced any of a list of a dozen or so problems associated with drinking, such as getting into fights after drinking or having shaky hands in the morning after drinking. Some number of these problems is then arbitrarily declared the cut-off point between alcoholics and non-alcoholics, so that any respondent who reports having experienced, say, five or more of these problems is defined as an 'alcoholic' whilst anyone reporting less than five is 'normal'. It is doubtful how far people defined as alcoholics by such a method are comparable to people admitted to mental hospitals for alcoholism treatment, since the latter often have a longish history of many severe interrelated problems from drinking. Although some overlap probably occurs, it would be almost certainly alarmist to project results of survey prevalence rates as evidence that there is some enormous hidden population that resembles people in treatment for alcoholism in every way except for their not being in treatment. Rather the discrepancy between the size of the survey defined alcoholic population and the clinically defined alcoholic population shows that there are probably many thousands of people experiencing various types of alcohol related problems who are not recognised by doctors or other agencies as having drinking problems, and who are not counted in numbers of alcoholics.

The Importance of Epidemiology

Confronted with all the difficulties over definition, it might appear that the epidemiologist would be well advised to abandon any attempt to estimate the incidence and prevalence of drinking problems. Such a resignation, however, would not be acceptable. Whatever the difficulties, it is important to pursue epidemiological research for two major reasons. Firstly, it is crucial to assess the size, distribution and severity of alcohol problems in order to help plan a proper and adequate response. It is essential to assess what sorts of problems, and of what severity, are associated with what sorts of consumption and drinking patterns before any meaningful consistent policy can be designed for preventive, educational and therapeutic needs. Secondly, epidemiology should not merely be a counting of heads; it should also involve the study of factors influencing the distribution of alcohol problems. This distribution, in turn, can provide clues as to how and why drinking problems develop. For example, the continually higher incidence of hospital admissions for alcoholism amongst the Scots and Irish compared to the English and Welsh suggests that cultural factors are influential in determining the prevalence of drinking problems. Epidemiology can thus assist our understanding of aetiology – the study of the causes and development of medical and social problems – which is discussed in Chapter 7.

When epidemiologists have kept these twin concerns uppermost, looking both for clues as to causation, and also seeking data on which to base plans for treatment and response strategies, then they have managed to go some way towards marrying the two worlds of alcohol problems.

Alcohol Consumption and Alcohol Problems

The most important development in this direction has been the accumulation of data which show that whatever the inconsistences in definition, a consistent relationship can be found between the prevalence of alcohol related problems (as indicated by rates of drunkenness convictions, liver cirrhosis mortality and hospital admissions for alcoholism) and the level of alcohol consumption.

The level of alcohol consumption in a population is usually expressed in terms of per capita consumption – the amount drunk by the average person. To estimate this, the total consumption of the population is firstly derived from production and sales figures of alcoholic beverages. It is then translated into an equivalent volume of absolute alcohol, based on the percentage volume of alcohol contained in each type of alcoholic drink. Per capita consumption is then simply derived by dividing the total national consumption of absolute alcohol by the number of people in the adult population.

The relationship between the level of per capita consumption and the prevalence of alcohol related problems was first noticed in periods when the availability of alcohol was suddenly reduced. The pattern was well illustrated in Britain during the First World War; when licensing hours reduced availability of alcohol, per capita consumption dropped markedly, and so did all the rates of alcohol related problems. Indeed, there was such a noticeable decline in alcoholic mortality and drunkenness that the Registrar General commented, 'it is difficult to avoid associating the two phenomena (consumption and mortality) as cause and effect.' (Wilson, 1939) The same phenomenon was observed in the USA during the Prohibition era when the incidence of liver cirrhosis was dramatically reduced.

After the Second World War, the relationship between consumption and problems was confirmed again, but this time by the two variables increasing together. Per capita consumption rose in most postwar societies, and invariably this was accompanied by increases in the prevalence of alcohol related problems. In England and Wales, this relationship commanded particular attention during the late 1960s and early 1970s when alcohol consumption and alcohol related problems accelerated so much that some commentators talked of an 'alcoholism explosion' (Merseyside, Lancashire & Cheshire Council on Alcoholism, 1975). Per capita consumption rose markedly throughout the 1960s, increasing 23 per cent between 1960 and 1969. It then took an even more dramatic upswing, rising 40 per cent between 1969 and 1974, when it seemed to level off on this new high plateau. This pattern of increase was thought to be related to the falls in the real price of alcohol as a proportion of disposable income and to changes in the availability and distribution of alcohol, such as the increase in number of supermarket outlets for alcoholic drinks.

Changes in the prevalence of alcohol related problems closely mirrored these trends in the pattern of availability and consumption. Convictions for drunkenness rose 11 per cent between 1960 and 1969, and then accelerated through a 27 per cent increase between 1969 and 1974. Hospital admissions for alcoholism rose 48 per cent in the five years before 1969, but 63 per cent in the five years following. As consumption stabilised from 1974 onwards, the increases in rates of alcohol related problems correspondingly decelerated. The number of persons found guilty of drinking and driving had increased an average of 23 per cent annually between 1969 and 1974, but only increased another 4 per cent in 1975. Since 1974 convictions for drunkenness itself have remained virtually static at around 21 per 10,000 of the population.

So despite all the vagaries in definition and difficulties in measurement, a clear pattern can be discerned. Both consumption and problems in England and Wales grew steadily throughout the 1960s, increased markedly between 1969 and 1974, and then remained at their newly elevated level. The years in which alcohol consumption increased the most were the same years in which the prevalence of alcohol related problems increased the most.

Theories of the Relationship Between Consumption and Problems

Why should this relationship hold so strongly? In the 1950s, the French epidemiologist Ledermann (1956) had tried to explain the relationship between per capita consumption and liver cirrhosis mortality by a statistical and mathematical theorem which claimed that a rise in average consumption inevitably meant a general move throughout the population towards heavier drinking. It was this generally heavier drinking, he assumed, which increased the likelihood of more drinkers suffering liver damage. An international review of epidemiological knowledge in 1975 (Bruun *et al.*, 1975) endorsed Ledermann's reasoning by assuming that alcohol related problems were concentrated amongst the heaviest drinkers, and that the higher the average consumption level, then the greater would be the number of these heavy drinkers. De Lint and Schmidt (1971) have compiled much evidence to support this theory and have concluded that 'the prevalence of alcoholism is invariably determined by the overall level of consumption in the population' — a statement which clearly illustrates how very forthright views on aetiology can arise from epidemiological research. From an aetiological viewpoint, the evidence collected by epidemiologists such as Ledermann and de Lint suggested that the number of people diagnosed as suffering from alcoholism — conceptualised by some as a permanent affliction — actually rose and fell with the amount of alcohol consumed within a society. It suggested that the size of the problem should not be conceived in terms of the number of people who were in some way pathologically inclined to become alcoholic. If there was a relationship between national consumption, individual consumption and problems, then we were, in a way, all at risk, and de Lint has been well aware that this represented a critique of the traditional disease perspective of alcoholism. Moreover, since de Lint and Schmidt have also indicated that per capita consumption was in turn inversely related to the price and availability of alcohol, they maintained that their theory had important implications for alcohol control policy. If they were correct to believe that a reduction in the availability of alcohol would always reduce per capita consumption, in turn reducing the number of heavy drinkers and the risk of people experiencing alcohol related problems, then the most efficient way of counteracting or preventing alcohol problems was simply to reduce availability, such as by increasing taxes on alcoholic drinks.

Not surprisingly, the alcoholic drinks industry has been disinclined to accept this theory, but there has also been a growing number of other critics with less vested interests. In the mid 1970s statisticians who re-examined the mathematical principles of the Ledermann-based theories found the underlying assumptions to be rather dubious (Miller & Agnew, 1974) and when Duffy (1977) examined the distributions of consumption amongst some general population samples, he found that they did not comply with the distributions predicted by Ledermann. Duffy concluded that, despite the evidence for a strong relationship between consumption and problems, explanations of this relationship reached by some epidemiologists were 'unjustified by their data', and that the theory that the distribution of alcohol consumption could be predicted from average consumption was 'illogical and contradicted by empirical evidence'. Such a critique undermined many popular assumptions about the epidemiology of alcohol problems, and was symptomatic of a quite distinct reorientation of focus. It confirmed the views of other epidemiologists who had felt all along that it was just too simplistic to believe that such a complex matter as the prevalence of alcohol related problems was really all determined by a single factor, the level of per capita consumption. This did not seem to allow for the individual circumstances of each drinker and for idiosyncratic risks and vulnerabilities. Surely there was more to the aetiology of drinking problems than how much people drank, and surely the problems of individual drinkers were not going to be prevented simply by raising the price of alcoholic drinks. Nevertheless, there still remained a massive amount of evidence showing a very strong relationship between consumption and problems.

What could be made of this paradox? Epidemiologists began to assume that there must be some validity in the relationship itself, but that the mathematical and statistical theories were not valid explanations of why the relationship held. They realised that there was a distinct need to consider in more detail the relationship between alcohol consumption and alcohol related problems and to discover the possible mechanisms operating behind gross figures, rather than just accepting the evidence of national statistics.

Difficulties in Using National Statistics

The validity of national statistics should always be viewed sceptically. The level of alcohol consumption cannot be estimated exactly from alcohol production and sales figures, which do not, for example, allow for the movement of retailed stock or for the consumption of home brewed alcohol. National statistics of alcohol related problems are also open to criticism. A rise in drunkenness arrests might not necessarily indicate more episodes of drunkenness, but simply a change in police policy, and as we have seen, hospital admissions for alcoholism probably only constitute a minority of the people with drinking problems. But the main shortcoming of national statistics is that they do not provide any clues as to the patterns which relate consumption to problems in particular groups and individuals. National trends might be made up of quite different patterns amongst different groups of drinkers. Unfortunately, it was only when Ledermann-based theories explaining the relationship between consumption and prevalence became exposed as equivocal that epidemiology's suspect preoccupation with national statistics became all too plain. Once national statistics were taken away, there was actually very little information left to suggest any alternative mechanisms which might explain the relationship. The most blatant deficiency was the lack of data on relationships over time between consumption and problems within particular groups and individuals, which can only be gleaned from studies of general population samples.

Fortunately, this situation is gradually being remedied. In particular, some indications of why alcohol related problems increased in England and Wales in the 1960s and 1970s can be gleaned from the analysis of two studies carried out in the same London suburb at two different times; the first in 1965 (Edwards *et al.*, 1972) and the second in 1974 (Cartwright *et al.*, 1975).

Survey Data on Increasing Consumption

Over the nine-year period, per capita consumption in the suburb increased 47 per cent and, as it happened, the increase in consumption was distributed in the way Ledermann would have predicted. That is, consumption had not increased so dramatically just because there were suddenly a few more very heavy drinkers, but rather because everyone had tended to increase their consumption. Yet the percentage of abstainers remained constant at 11 per cent, and people did not drink on any more days of the week in 1974 than they had in 1965. Rather the major change was that on a drinking day in 1974, 'average drinkers' consumed 56 per cent more alcohol than they would have done in 1965.

This fitted in with the thinking of Scandinavian epidemiologists who had pointed out that even major increases in per capita consumption had not usually created new drinking patterns. Usually they had been superimposed onto existing patterns. This 'addition hypothesis' (Makëla, 1975) implies that new ways of drinking do not displace old ones, but rather add new elements to them. Sulkunen (1976) has pointed out that these additions to the existing drinking patterns comprise new consumer groups, new drinking situations, and new ways of drinking. Examples of each element within the changing drinking patterns in Britain would be that young women became an important consumer group; they became more likely to go into public houses unaccompanied by men, and they tended to experiment with a wider range of drinks than previously. Yet despite these innovations, the major elements of British drinking patterns remained stable. Overall, for example, most alcohol continued to be consumed in the form of beer. This hypothesis, in conjunction with the London survey data, suggested that the relationship between consumption and problems observed over the years to be 'apparently fixed', was not fixed because of the statistical logic of Ledermann's hypothesis, but because the stability of the underlying drinking patterns determined how increased consumption was distributed. To investigate this possibility, the London surveys were then examined to discover any changes in the prevalence of problems which might have accompanied the redistribution of consumption.

Survey Data on Increasing Problems

In both London studies, respondents were asked whether they had recently experienced any of a series of alcohol related problems. The same relationship was found in both samples, the greater an individual's consumption, the more likely he was to report having experienced alcohol related problems. Although this consistent overall correlation was what one would expect from the studies of national statistics, the survey data showed this to be only part of the story. For behind this relationship, there existed considerable variation between different groups and individuals. Individuals drinking the same amount reported different numbers of problems. For example, as a group, young middle-class males drank the same amount in a week as did older upper-class males. Yet the young males reported an average of three times more problems than the older males. Closer investigation of this data showed that in the individual cases, the relationship between consumption and problems was mediated by two major factors – the person's drinking pattern and his personal characteristics. The consumption of the middle-class young male was concentrated on fewer days of the week than that of the upper-class older male. And whenever two demographic groups in the sample drank the same amount, the group who consumed more *per drinking day* reported a higher average number of problems. Although this suggests spreading consumption over more days of the week may carry less risk of suffering the problems which happened to be measured in the London survey, other alcohol related problems might be more associated with other types of drinking patterns. For example, other studies have shown that frequent moderate consumption is more likely than occasional heavy drinking to cause liver cirrhosis (Rankin *et al.*, 1975). Yet both sets of studies concur in indicating that there are probably relationships between specific types of drinking patterns and the development of particular alcohol related problems.

The second intermediary factor between the level of consumption and the prevalence of problems appeared to be personal characteristics which made some people more vulnerable than others to developing problems, even when their consumption and drinking pattern was the same. This finding appeals to common sense, since there must be many variables explaining why one person is more likely than another to experience more problems from the same level of consumption consumed in the same way. An individual's vulnerability to alcohol related problems depends, for example, on whether he has a family or not, whether he can drive or not, what age he is, what weight he is, what sort of occupation he has, and what his previous drinking behaviour has been like.

Implications for Treatment and Prevention

The survey evidence thus clearly demonstrates that the prevalence of drinking problems *does* relate to the level of consumption, but that this should not be interpreted as deterministic evidence of some inexorable relationship between consumption and problems in every case. It is not possible to assert that any specific level of consumption is definitely likely to cause problems. We cannot claim, for example, that if a person drinks, say, half a bottle of whisky a day, he will definitely suffer problems. However, we can say that the more a person drinks, the greater risk he runs of experiencing drinking problems. We can also say that his risk of experiencing particular problems will be greater if he drinks in certain patterns, or if he is particularly vulnerable to developing certain problems because of his physical, psychological and social characteristics.

The reconceptualised view of the aetiology of alcohol related problems could be represented diagrammatically in Figure 6.1.

Davies has recognised that such a theory implies it would be more rational to treat people with drinking problems in terms of the factors which led them to drink excessively, and in terms of risk associated with their particular drinking pattern and their personal vulnerability. The question would then become not, 'Is this man an alcoholic or not?'

Figure 6.1: The Aetiology of Alcohol Related Problems

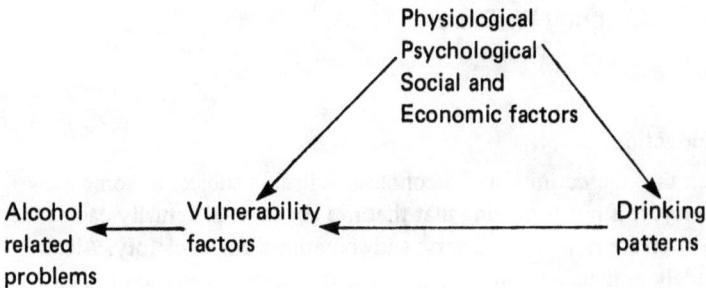

Physiological
Psychological
Social and
Economic factors

Alcohol   Vulnerability   Drinking
related   factors   patterns
problems

but rather 'What factors operate in his case which make him drink so much and therefore what can I do to help him in the future to deal with those particular factors?' (Davies, 1977)

Thus epidemiology has begun to move into areas which will help to develop a rationale for approaches to conceptualisation and treatment. To realise the potential of this new direction, epidemiology will need to make much closer examination of the relationships between an individual's consumption pattern, his vulnerability and the development of drinking problems. In conclusion, however, it should be noted that although epidemiology is now heading in this more sophisticated direction, the new theories and data still reaffirm the basic principle of alcohol control policy. It remains true that, given the stability of drinking patterns, reducing alcohol availability will be likely to decrease consumption and hence reduce the prevalence of alcohol related problems. Nevertheless, future epidemiology in this area too should pursue the more sophisticated task of outlining a detailed strategy for prevention, by determining *in which ways* and *to what extent* alcohol should be controlled to produce *what size* of reduction *in which* particular alcohol related problems.

7 THE CAUSES OF ALCOHOLISM

Anthony W. Clare

Introduction

Given that the definition of alcoholism is itself a subject of some controversy, it is not surprising that theories about what actually causes the condition are numerous, diverse and sometimes contradictory. Alcohol is widely available in most cultures and thus any explanation has to account for that which differentiates those drinkers, the minority, who become alcoholics from those drinkers, the majority, who do not. Many attempts to provide such an explanation have been made but to date no single explanatory theory has proven adequate. Indeed, partly as a consequence of this failure, many experts subscribe to the view that there is no single cause and that alcoholism is best envisaged as a condition in which several causal factors operate to produce the final clinical picture. The major explanatory models are discussed in detail below but it is important to bear in mind that while many of these theories contain useful insights concerning the nature of alcoholism at the present time, none can be considered in isolation from the others.

Any explanation of alcoholism needs to take into account the particular properties of the drug that is alcohol, the constitution and personality of the individual consuming the drug and the social and cultural milieu in which alcohol use and abuse occur. Each of the three major categories of aetiological theories lays special emphasis on one of these three factors. *Biological* models of alcoholism primarily focus on the pharmacological properties of alcohol and its effects on the central nervous system. The alcoholic tends to be portrayed as a person who, by virtue of some hitherto unexplained disturbance in his ability to metabolise alcohol normally or some particular sensitivity to alcohol or one or more of its break-down products, is constitutionally predisposed to develop physiological dependence on the substance. *Psychological* theories tend to rest on the assumption that alcoholics share certain personality traits or tendencies believed to be of crucial importance in the development of the disorder. Such a view has led in the past to attempts to describe the so-called 'alcoholic personality', i.e. a constellation of traits, attitudes and aptitudes thought to constitute a specific psychological vulnerability to develop alcoholism. More recently, psychological theorists have turned their attention to the manner in

which individuals learn to use and misuse alcohol and the view of alcoholism as a learned piece of maladaptive behaviour has consequently
gained ground. The third category of explanatory theories goes outside
the drug and the individual to explore the strong empirical relationship
that exists between socio-cultural variables and the incidence of alcohol
use, abuse and dependence. In the view of those who advance this *socio-
cultural* model of alcoholism, the reasons why a person drinks, and
hence the reasons why he abuses drink, are primarily sociological and
anthropological rather than psychological or medical.

Biological Causes

The earliest biological models of alcohol dependence tended to suggest
that the circumstance of intoxication was itself a necessary and a
sufficient reason to explain the remorseless spiral toward ever increasing
drinking, craving, tolerance, dependence and harm. Within the framework of such explanations, the potent addictive properties of alcohol
were emphasised, and in particular the tissue tolerance, withdrawal
symptoms, subjective craving, apparent loss of control over consumption and the steady physical and mental deterioration. Much research
has been directed at detecting biochemical, physiological and neuro-
physiological abnormalities to explain the mechanisms of alcohol addiction, but the great bulk of such research has tended to be concerned
with individuals already heavily dependent on alcohol. Thus, while a
number of possible disturbances in physical functioning have been
reported in alcoholics, there is much uncertainty about the actual
causal status of such abnormalities since they may be as much the
consequences of alcohol abuse as its antecedents.

Metabolic Causes

The search for some metabolic defect in individuals physiologically
dependent on alcohol is constant but to date has not been particularly
fruitful. Alcoholics have been reported to metabolise alcohol at a faster
rate than non-alcoholics while other physiological and biochemical
measures claimed to differentiate alcoholic from non-alcoholic populations include sleep patterns, salivary flow, glucose metabolism and the
excretion of certain metabolic products in the urine. In all of these
instances, the alcoholic population studied by researchers showed
abnormalities that were altered in the direction of normality following
the ingestion of alcohol. This has led to a suggestion that alcohol exercises a 'normalising' effect in alcoholics; that is to say, in a dry state the
alcoholic's physical state is thought to differ significantly from that of

non-alcoholic controls, but when drinking this state moves back to normality. If such physiological or biochemical differences between alcoholics and non-alcoholics could be shown to antedate the onset of alcohol dependence, then this would indeed be powerful evidence in favour of the view that alcohol has a unique functional value to the incipient alcoholic. However, once again it has to be acknowledged that such differences may well be the result rather than the cause of excessive alcohol ingestion and until there is conclusive evidence to demonstrate the proper causal sequence this 'normalising' theory will remain a speculative explanation.

Neurotransmitter Alterations

In recent years there has been much interest in substances occurring in different parts of the brain which are concerned with the transmission of impulses or messages from one brain cell to another. These neuro-transmitters are known to play a role in certain psychiatric disorders, such as anxiety and depression, and are also affected by drugs, such as the tranquillisers, used to treat such disorders. In man, alcohol is known to cause alterations in neurotransmitter function and it has been suggested that such alterations may be related to the development of tolerance to alcohol and to the appearance of withdrawal symptoms. A related theory suggests that derivatives of neurotransmitters and of alcohol might occur during chronic alcohol ingestion and that such compounds might act on centres in the brain rather like the metabolic products of morphine and other opiates are believed to act on specific opiate receptors in the brains of seriously drug dependent individuals. The discovery of naturally occurring morphine-like substances (enkephalins) acting on morphine receptors in the brain and exerting a powerful analgesic effect has provoked a new enthusiasm amongst researchers anxious to clarify the physiological basis of drug and alcohol dependence.

Genetic Factors

Given that the rates of alcoholism are much increased among the relatives of alcoholics compared with the general population, the question arises as to whether genetic mechanisms are involved in the condition. There have been reports of associations between alcoholism and known inherited characteristics or 'genetic markers', such as colour blindness, of preference for alcohol in genetic strains of mice, and of an increased incidence of alcoholism among adopted individuals with a known alcoholic biological parent from whom they were separately reared. Human populations have been found to differ in their responses to alcohol, for reasons that are clearly not entirely cultural. For example, Koreans, Chinese and Japanese become flushed more often than Caucasians after small oral doses of alcohol. Furthermore, there are differences between populations in the relative frequency of various types of the enzyme, alcohol dehydrogenase, which is crucially involved in the metabolic breakdown of alcohol in the body. There are also reported differences in the rate whereby ethnic groups eliminate alcohol from the blood.

To date, alternative explanations to the genetic one for such various phenomena have not been disproved. There are also those who argue, like Pattison (1974), that on intuitive grounds alcoholism seems too complex a behaviour pattern to be explained solely by genetic determinants or biological defects. However, in a recent detailed view of the subject, Shields (1977) concluded that despite many uncertainties and inconsistencies, there is growing evidence 'that genetic factors, some general, others perhaps relatively specific, are probably involved (along with others) in the development of alcoholism in man.'

Psychological Causes

An influential explanatory model in the field of alcoholism is that which derives its theoretical framework from classic psychoanalytical theory. This theory locates the source of problem drinking within the individual's psychological make-up. Derived from such a position is the idea of the 'alcoholic personality', a personality type vulnerable to alcohol and prone to develop alcohol dependence. An alternative psychological view is that derived from behavioural theory. According to this view, alcoholism, like any other deviant behaviour or symptom, is the result of maladaptive learning and must be corrected by a process of retraining. A strikingly different view again, derived from the principles of transactional analysis, explains alcoholism as a game, a consciously adopted stratagem which enables the alcoholic (and those around him) to cope with his and their personalities, difficulties and interactions.

Psychoanalytic Theories of Causation

Psychoanalysts define addiction in terms of a dependence on a substance, an activity or a person which is believed to provide pleasure on the one hand and relief from psychic pain or anxiety on the other. Such a dependence is conceived of as resulting from a failure of personality development on the part of the addict. Addiction is seen as a protective defence against graver consequences of such a failure, such as suicide, psychosis, asocial or criminal behaviour. This double function of the addictions led some analysts to place them midway between the neuroses (conceptualised as attempts to avoid psychic pain) and the perversions (attempts to obtain pleasure). From the psychoanalytic viewpoint, alcoholism can be considered to be a substitute for emotionally mature adaptation, as a means of coping with conflicts and as the result of a variety of specific failures in emotional growth. Some analysts stress the aspects of general dependency exhibited by many alcoholics and relate it to unresolved conflicts over parental relationships in early childhood. Other analysts emphasise the element of modelling in child-parent relationships. The adult alcoholic's pathological behaviour is seen to reflect actual pathological recollections of what his parents were like as well as false recollections based on childhood fantasies and impressions. The so-called ego-defence methods employed by the alcoholic, namely the denial of unpleasant reality, the projection of blame, are viewed as relating to the inability to delay the gratification of impulses and drives. The alcoholic is seen as an economically and emotionally dependent person, passive and lacking in perseverance, devoid of interest in achieving anything other than immediate pleasure or relief. His love relationships are characterised by a self-centredness, a clinging to mothering persons and depressive moods when such support is not forthcoming.

The major problem with such an explanatory theory is that it is too all-embracing. While it is true that alcoholism is a pathological condition characterised by immature functioning, regression and denial are also associated with a number of other forms of psychiatric illness and deviant behaviour. Why does alcoholism develop in some and not in others? Moreover the disinhibiting effects of alcohol that facilitate the overt expression of repressed feelings and regressed behaviour are commonly observed among drinkers who have not progressed to alcohol abuse and dependence. Similarly, while the disruptive experiences of early childhood may increase vulnerability to the development of alcoholism, they are far from specific to alcoholism but are reported in a wide variety of psychopathological conditions. Finally, there is the very serious shortcoming of such theories, remarked upon by critics of psychoanalysis, namely that they are difficult to disprove. It is impossible to disprove the immaturity of the alcoholic personality since his alcoholism is evidence of it and all the explanations of the genesis of that personality are retrospectively based.

Personality Theories

For many years, attempts have been made to delineate a consistent set of personality attributes that correlate with the development of alcoholism. However, despite a wealth of studies, no specific personality traits have been linked to alcoholic individuals. In so far as unusual or abnormal traits have been found, they have been attributed to the effect of alcohol abuse with as much ease as they have been blamed for its cause. The best evidence for the causal status of trait variables in the development of alcoholism is to be found in longitudinal studies of personality, but these are relatively rare. In one celebrated study, Jones (1968) reported on the personality characteristics of six cases out of 66 boys studied during childhood who subsequently manifested 'problem drinking'. These six boys were reportedly uncontrolled, impulsive and rebellious during childhood but the small numbers in the study suggest caution in interpreting the results. Another study (McCord & McCord, 1962), this time of 255 boys followed up over 18 years, found 29 who manifested alcohol problems on the occasion of the follow-up. When their childhood records were matched with a control group of non-alcoholic boys, early personality traits of unrestrained aggression, hyperactivity, denial of childhood fears and of inferiority feelings ('hypermasculinity') were identified to a significantly greater extent in the alcoholic subjects' childhood assessments.

A related explanation involves the fact that alcohol acts as a potent tranquilliser for highly anxious individuals. There is some support for the view that some alcoholics manifest high levels of anxiety and that alcohol has depressant and sedative pharmacological properties. In addition, studies have demonstrated that the precipitating occasion for the onset of drinking episodes in alcoholics is often the occurrence of heightened anxiety. However, there is still insufficient evidence in favour of the view that anxiety is more prevalent among alcoholics than among other groups of disturbed individuals for whom alcohol has not become an important method of coping. Nonetheless, many alcoholics do spontaneously list as one of their main motivations for drinking the fact that alcohol does provide a tranquillising effect.

Another view suggests that alcoholics are individuals who suffer from pervasive feelings of inferiority which result in an enhanced need for power in the face of inadequate personality resources to achieve it. In the face of frustrated ambitions, the alcoholic resorts to drinking to achieve a sense of self-satisfaction and achievement as well as a release from tension. To date, this striving for power formulation remains an interesting but unsupported hypothesis.

Behavioural Theories

A relatively simple psychological theory of alcoholism is that based on behavioural principles. Alcoholic behaviour is understood to be caused and maintained by the simple association of drinking with a positive and rewarding experience. Alcoholism is regarded as a conditioned behavioural response that can be 'unlearned' through the appropriate modification of environmental stimuli and reinforcement situations. More complex theories acknowledge that alcohol abuse is a highly complicated form of behaviour. However, the major assumption remains the same, namely that alcoholics begin and continue drinking because alcohol ingestion is followed by a fall in anxiety, stress or tension.

A two-stage model to explain the genesis of excessive drinking has been suggested by Bandura (1969). In this view, the positive value of alcohol initially derives from the central depressant and anaesthetic properties of the substance. Thus, individuals who are subjected to stressful situations may obtain relief from stress through drinking alcohol due to its pharmacological effects. The behaviour of drinking is reinforced by the reduction of unpleasant experience that follows from it. Repeated experiences in which the drinking of alcohol leads to a reduction of anxiety, stress or other aversive stimuli results in a progressive strengthening of the alcohol habits. Once established, the excessive use of alcohol begins to have aversive effects on the individual that in turn set up renewed stimulus conditions for continued drinking. Eventually, with prolonged heavy drinking, physiological alterations occur in the body resulting in physiological dependence. As a consequence of this development, the distressing withdrawal symptoms themselves become the stimulus conditions for alcohol consumption. In second-stage conditioning, drinking is reinforced automatically and continually through the alleviation and termination of withdrawal symptoms which it provides.

Support for such a tension-reducing hypothesis has been obtained from animal studies. Howeve, reliance on tension and its reduction as a sole causal factor is not warranted by the facts. Other behavioural factors may have aetiological significance however. Social reinforcement, such as peer approval, or imitative behaviour, for example of parental drinking attitudes and habits, may serve to initiate and/or maintain excessive drinking. This question has been discussed at greater length in Chapter 4. More recent behavioural approaches to alcoholism have tended to see the specific antecedents and reinforcers of excessive drinking as highly variable from individual to individual. Such theorists argue that a careful analysis of the precise stimulus-response-reinforcement relationships in each individual case is essential for any understanding of aetiology. The implications of this and other behaviour views for prevention and treatment will be discussed in Chapter 12.

Alcoholism as 'Game'

Some theorists, drawing on the concepts employed in transactional analysis, have argued that alcoholism, like other forms of deviant behaviour, is best understood as a 'game', i.e. a complicated series of transactions engaged in with the purpose of obtaining an interpersonal advantage. By postulating that alcoholics play a game, it is implied that alcoholism should be understood as a sequence of interpersonal moves with an ulterior motive or 'pay-off' rather than as an addiction, illness or psychological defect. Steiner (1969) has even gone so far as to identify three distinct 'games'. There is the 'aggressive' game wherein the alcoholic puts himself in a position of being obviously disapproved of and allows those who disapprove to appear virtuous and blameless. The specific thesis of the game is 'you're good, I'm bad, try and stop me'. It is suggested that the alcoholic player is basically interested in making persecuting parental figures so angry that they show their impotence and foolishness. There is the 'self-damaging' game usually played with a partner who is unable to or has great difficulty in provoding emotional or sexual support. As a consequence, the alcoholic's continued drinking is to the partner's advantage since as long as the drinking continues, the partner's own emotional deficiency and his part in the game will not be exposed. The third game, based on tissue self-destruction, is characterised by the alcoholic obtaining satisfaction (or 'strokes' as transactional analysts term them) by making himself physically ill. By sacrificing his bodily integrity, he forces others to take care of him. The 'pay-off' in this game is the provision of medical care and treatment, nursing attention and accommodation.

The attractiveness of such conceptualisations of alcoholism is that they provide some useful insights into its phenomena. However, caution needs to be exercised in handling them. Once again, it is the behaviour of the alcoholic and those close to him *after* he has developed his alcoholism which forms the foundation of the explanatory theory. Many of the interactions observed by behavioural analysts result from the alcohol misuse and cannot logically be identified as causes of the condition. The other problem with such approaches is that they embody a strong moralistic and punitive flavour hardly warranted by the evidence marshalled to support their validity.

Socio-cultural Causes

The facilitating effect of certain cultural factors on the development of alcoholism is well recognised. Mortality rates from cirrhosis of the liver vary greatly from country to country. Schmidt (1977) points out that rate differences among general populations of such magnitude usually indicate *a priori* the importance of environmental influences in the aetiology of the disease. Since the rate of death from cirrhosis due to factors other than alcohol use has varied very little over the last 20 years in most Western countries, such changes as are found in cirrhosis mortality can be attributed to changes in the number of chronic heavy users of alcoholic beverages. Over the past two decades, cirrhosis mortality has been increasing at a steady and often rapid rate in many parts of the world. During this same period, the idea that the rate of any alcohol related problem in a population is related to the per capita level of alcohol consumption in that population has gained ground. This hypothesis has been discussed at greater length in Chapter 6. Such a view shifts the search for *causes* of alcoholism away from the individual's psychopathology and biochemistry and towards those factors, potentially within society's grasp, which may influence overall consumption rates.

Occupational Factors

Occupation appears to be an important causal factor in alcoholism. Working in the drink trade itself, as a barman, publican, wine merchant or brewer, places the individual at a high risk, but others including seamen, printers, salesmen, businessmen and doctors tend to manifest high rates of alcoholism. Predisposing effects include the availability of cheap or free alcohol, strong peer pressure to drink, a lack of super-vision at work and separation from normal social or sexual relationships.

Ethnic Factors

Ethnic and subcultural differences in the use and abuse of alcohol suggest that pre-alcoholic learning factors in the development of alco-holism are important. That is to say, the proper and controlled use of alcoholic beverages is dependent on underlying attitudes towards alcohol and mores regulating drinking practices. Children are socialized into culturally established attitudes, beliefs and practices regarding alcohol consumption. Thus the extremely low rates of alcoholism reported among Jews, Moslems and Mormons, for example, can be accounted for by the cultural prohibitions against the use or abuse of the drug formulated by these groups. Certain countries, including Scot-

land, Ireland and the United States, have been characterised as ambivalent cultures, that is to say they have contradictory attitudes towards
the use of alcohol and oscillate between a permissive tolerance of
drunkenness and heavy drinking and a moral denunciation of physiological dependence. Permissive cultures, where attitudes towards the
use of alcohol are favourable, but where there are strong and consistent
social sanctions against intoxication, drunkenness or other forms of
deviant drinking, have also been noted and examples are to be found in
Spain, Italy and Portugal. An over-permissive culture, in which the
attitudes towards drinking are favourable and are also favourable to
other forms of deviant behaviour while drinking, is that of France. In
general, those ethnic groups with a permissive yet moderate attitude
towards alcohol and a system of firm, consistent and acknowledged
social sanctions against its misuse, have low rates of alcoholism and low
rates of alcohol related problems. These issues have been discussed at
greater length in Chapter 3.

Familial Factors

Socio-cultural factors may also operate through familial mechanisms.
Family studies from Sweden, Switzerland and the United States all
agree in finding very much higher rates of alcoholism in the parents and
siblings of alcoholics than those thought most appropriate for the
general population. As we have seen, a genetic factor may be operating
but one reason for doubting that this is the only explanation is the high
rate often reported for relatives genetically one degree less close than
parents or siblings and on average only sharing 25 per cent and not 50
per cent of their genes with the affected individual. Genetic theories, in
contrast, predict much lower risks for second-degree than first-degree
relatives. A number of familial behaviour patterns have been
implicated in the transmission of alcoholism. Parental conflict about
drinking, parental disagreement and ambiguity concerning drinking
practices and parental abuse of alcohol have all been noted by observers.
Paternal punitiveness and paternal escapist reactions to crisis were identified by McCord and McCord (1962) in their study of the family backgrounds of male alcoholics. It has even been claimed (Cahalan & Room,
1974) that problem drinking among males can be predicted quite
effectively using only the traditional variables of age, socio-economic
status, urbanisation, ethnic origin and religious affiliation. O'Connor's
detailed study (1978) of drinking practices in two ethnic groups,
English and Irish young drinkers, lends considerable substance to the
view that it is parental attitudes towards alcohol as perceived by the

young and the effect of peer pressures which constitute the important ethnic factors concerned with alcohol intake, reducing still further the claims for the more traditional view that it is constitutional factors of a metabolic or psychological variety which are important.

Stress

Social, cultural and familial factors may also operate by increasing or aggravating conditions of environmental stress that provoke or precipitate episodes of alcohol abuse. Alcoholism has been reported to develop during periods of crisis or following significant life events which have led to serious instability, confusion and role stress. For example, women who have commenced excessive drinking in their late thirties and early forties have attributed the onset of their drinking problems to alterations in their roles as wife and mother, alterations which may include the menopause, loss of husband, and children leaving home. Other instances of stress include marital disharmony, unemployment and death of a relative. It is suggested that during such periods of heightened stress, an individual's normal coping mechanisms are overwhelmed and he or she resorts to more extreme means of easing the stress including, in some cases, heavy consumption of alcohol.

High rates of separation and divorce have been reported among alcoholics and some commentators have interpreted this as evidence of disabling psychological factors in the personality structure of the alcoholic. It has been argued that the social behaviour of the alcoholic alternates between cycles of sociability and alienation, a pattern which makes the maintenance of normal marital relationships difficult. Others have blamed the high marital failure rate on the alcoholic's poor choice of a spouse, arising out of strong dependency needs or fantasies of acquiring power. However, such explanations apart, it seems reasonable to hold that the presence of alcoholism in a marital partner might by itself constitute a sufficient incentive to divorce or separation. Once again, we are confronted by the problem that it is as easy and as reasonable to identify an explanation, in this case the idea of crisis or stress, as an *effect* of alcoholism as it is to identify it as a possible *cause*.

Availability of Alcohol

The idea that it is alcohol that causes alcoholism needs both attention and qualification. Until recently, such a view tended to be somewhat neglected in favour of the notion that alcohol consumption of heavy drinkers or alcoholics is symptomatic of a distinct disorder and the problem regarded as drunkenness not drinking and alcoholism not alcohol. This position has always been favoured by the alcohol industry and was tersely formulated in a submission to the Canadian Government by the Association of Canadian Distillers (1973): 'Alcohol and alcoholism are two entirely different subjects — while alcoholism is a major health problem, alcohol is not. Just as sugar is not the cause of diabetes, alcohol is not the cause of alcoholism.' Such a view is now being contested by those who argue that there is a direct relationship between per capita consumption in a population and the extent of excessive and problem-related consumption in that same population (Schmidt & de Lint, 1972). In turn, the factors known to have a bearing on per capita consumption include the real price of the alcoholic beverages in question and prices of related commodities that serve as substitutes or complements, changes in taste as reflected in trends in beverage preferences and the value of what economists have termed 'personal disposable income', i.e. that income left to the individual when taxes and basic food and other requirements have been taken care of.

There is mounting evidence that international and regional differences in rates of death from liver cirrhosis are very closely associated with differences in the apparent per capita consumption of alcoholic beverages. When the availability of alcohol has been curtailed, as happened in France during the Second World War, there has been a dramatic fall in cirrhosis mortality. Between 1954 and 1973, alcohol consumption and cirrhosis mortality rates in the United Kingdom have risen in parallel. While a relatively high level of general consumption of alcohol does not necessarily imply a high prevalence of heavy users and abusers and conversely a lower per capita consumption does not preclude the existence of higher rates of alcoholism, the relationship between consumption levels and the proportion of problem drinkers in a given population is such as to suggest to a number of researchers that one significant response to the growing problem of alcoholism may well lie in the adoption of stricter controls over the licensing, retailing, taxing and advertising of alcoholic beverages.

Conclusion

The majority of contemporary researchers in the area of alcoholism espouse a multifaceted approach to the study of causes of alcohol abuse and dependence. Such an approach incorporates elements from the broad areas of psychology, physiology and sociology. One such model has been summarised by Plaut (1967) and is quoted in the survey of current theories of causation contained in the Rand Report on alcoholism and treatment:

> A tentative model may be developed for understanding the causes of problem drinking, even though the precise roles of the various factors have not yet been determined. An individual who, 1) responds to beverage alcohol in a certain way, perhaps physiologically determined, by experiencing intense relief and relaxation, and who, 2) has certain personality characteristics, such as difficulty in dealing with and overcoming depression, frustration, and anxiety, and who, 3) is a member of a culture in which there is both pressure to drink and culturally induced guilt and confusion regarding what kinds of drinking behaviour are appropriate, is more likely to develop trouble than will most other persons. An intermingling of certain factors may be necessary for the development of problem drinking, and the relative importance of the differential causal factors no doubt varies from one individual to another.

The implications of such a view for the understanding and treatment of alcoholism are obvious. With a simple disease model of alcoholism which envisages the cause of alcoholism as an organically-based defect rendering the alcoholic vulnerable to alcohol, the therapeutic solution is a strict adherence to an abstinence regime pending some medical breakthrough aimed at remedying the defect. A view of alcoholism as learned maladaptive behaviour, on the other hand, holds out the possibility of retraining some alcoholics to drink socially and responsibly. An emphasis on socio-cultural causation directs attention to such factors as the availability of alcohol in society, its advertising, marketing and retailing, the societal value placed on its consumption, the manner in which alcohol use is initiated and maintained, the relative cost of the substance and the legal controls on its use and abuse. It seems clear that a proper and comprehensive approach to the treatment of alcoholism needs to reflect the multifactorial approach that is now implicit in current theories of causation advanced by most theorists in this area.

8 ALCOHOL AND THE FAMILY
Jim Orford

Introduction

Looking back, most people would find it almost impossible to recollect their earliest memories of alcohol. But the chances are that they were conveyed within the family. Perhaps it meant important occasions when visitors came, or special celebrations. Perhaps it was associated with father being unusually playful, or with mother being unusually angry. Perhaps its mention was associated with gleeful laughter, or with tension and gloom, or perhaps it was accepted as a daily matter-of-fact affair. Perhaps it was on the kitchen table daily in bottles, or perhaps it came out of a forbidden part of the sideboard only rarely. Perhaps it was not allowed at home at all.

Very little is known about children's early perceptions of the use of alcohol in their families. The known evidence has been discussed in Chapter 4. It is known that the consumption of wine in Britain went up between five- and sixfold between the early 1950s and the early 1970s, so children of the present generation presumably witness their parents drinking wine with meals that much more frequently than was true a generation ago. It is also known from many surveys that have been carried out in Europe, North America and elsewhere that the general trend is for the amount of young people's drinking to be correlated with that of their parents. This is, however, only a broad general trend which is true for smoking and for other social habits. There is a suggestion from some of these surveys that in cases where the family provides no moderate model of drinking for a young person to follow, or where a young person is in rebellion against parental values and attitudes, that there is a greater risk of excessive or immoderate drinking. These are just some amongst a variety of unrelated facts and suggestions, most departing little from common sense, which we possess about the relatively normal use of alcohol in the family. As is true of much of the alcohol studies field, there is much more information on the abnormal than the normal. This chapter will concentrate on alcoholism in the family, bearing in mind that we have only a rough and ready picture of the normal role of alcohol and the family against which to compare it.

The Impact of Alcoholism on Marriage

We must begin by looking at the impact of alcoholism on the marital pair in isolation. This topic has in fact been examined more closely than any other. Children and other family members have tended to be neglected, although recently more attention has been placed on the impact of alcoholism on children — a topic which will be considered in a later section of this chapter.

Alcoholism as a Source of Stress

One of the most straightforward ways of viewing alcoholism and marriage is to view alcoholism as a condition that arises in one member of the family and creates stress for other family members, especially for the drinker's spouse. According to this view the problem is located firmly in the condition suffered by one member of the family. Like the disease concept of alcoholism, with which this view fits most happily, it probably represents a gross oversimplification although there may be much merit in it. A quite different way of looking at the matter will be presented in a later section of this chapter. The simple model may indeed fit the facts better for some families than for others.

Jackson's article (1954) was an influential contribution which appeared to take this view of alcoholism as a source of stress. She made detailed observations at meetings of Al-Anon, the organisation associated with Alcoholics Anonymous but for relatives of alcoholics (in practice mainly wives), and also took histories from wives recruited from a variety of other sources. On this basis she outlined seven successive stages through which she considered that families passed in making an adjustment to the crisis of alcoholism in the family.

There are two main comments that must be made about Jackson's ideas. The first is that subsequent research has shown them to be over-elaborate. Although individual families may be only too painfully aware of a progression that has occurred in their own problems over a period of time, the progression is not the same in different families, and the same progression may take a shorter or longer time in different families. Nevertheless, there do appear to be two broad and fairly distinct stages in family life associated with a worsening alcohol problem in the husband. Family recognition of the problem, first attempts by wives to control drinking, social isolation of the family and transfer of part of the husband's family role to the wife generally occur at an earlier stage than fearful reactions on the part of a wife, her feelings of hopelessness about being able to cope with the problem, decline or ceasing of marital sexual behaviour, and the seeking of outside help.

The second point about Jackson's paper is that it concerns only drinking husbands and their non-alcoholic wives. We cannot generalise to marriages where the wife is the problem drinker. Indeed almost all the research that has been done on alcoholism and marriage has concerned alcoholic husbands and their wives, and we can really only speculate about how similar or different is the picture when the problem is the other way about.

Marriage Roles

A major complaint of those who live with people with serious drinking problems is that the latter are not around enough or do not pull their weight. The present author's study (Orford *et al.*, 1976) of wives married to problem drinking husbands in London, showed this up quite clearly. Complaints were made over things large and small. Many husbands were less involved in housework, or in doing repairs around the home than either they or their wives considered ideal. Many were generally accused of not 'being around when needed by the family'. Interestingly, although there was a general under-involvement in family 'tasks', there was no such under-involvement (indeed in some cases a suggestion of over-influence) in family 'decisions' about social and recreational life and about marital sexual behaviour.

Again two points can be made about such studies, and again both of them serve to put the study of alcohol and the family in a wider context or to help guard us against oversimplification. The first concerns the great variation which is to be found between families that contain an alcohol problem. Although the general trends may be for wives to complain about their drinking husbands doing too little, there are many cases where this factor is less important, and instances come to mind of husbands with drinking problems who were more than usually involved in the day-to-day running of their homes. Alcohol dependence is far from being a fixed entity which takes invariant form, and it is not surprising to find that family patterns associated with it are highly varied. There may be general trends but there are no simple generalisations.

Secondly, there is no reason to suppose that the findings on marriage roles are peculiar to alcohol problems. Studies of families in which husbands had quite other forms of psychological distress have produced very similar results.

Dissatisfaction, Disturbance and Dissolution

There can be little doubt that wives married to men with serious drinking problems often experience hardship of greater or lesser degree. The following are the number of wives, out of the 100 involved in the Orford study, who made each of ten complaints about their husband's behaviour:

Restlessness or wakefulness at night	74	Ever attempted to injure you seriously	27
Allowing himself to get dirty, unkempt or smelly	61	Going on and on for hours rowing with you	57
Failing to join in family activities	65	Breaking furniture, windows, ornaments, etc.	49
Picking quarrels with you	76	Extreme possessiveness and jealousy towards you	49
Sometimes threatening you	72		
Ever beaten you	45		

Inevitably the hardship takes its toll in terms of the spouse's disturbance. Many wives report being drawn into a nightmarish spiral of tension, deceit, guilt and uncertainty about their own part in causing the problems and in responding to them. When groups of wives of problem drinkers have been given objective tests of personality disturbance, the usual finding is that they show a generally raised level of distress. Bailey (1962) asked wives of problem drinkers a series of questions about psychosomatic symptoms which had previously been used in one of the largest ever community surveys of mental health — the Midtown Manhatten Survey in New York. Of all married women in the Midtown Survey, 35 per cent had appeared to be at least moderately disturbed. In comparison, 65 per cent of wives in Bailey's study who were at the time living with a husband who was drinking excessively were at least moderately disturbed, and 43 per cent of wives living with a husband whose drinking had previously been excessive but which was no longer so, were at least moderately disturbed. Wives who had previously lived with excessively drinking husbands, but who were no longer doing so either because their husband had stopped drinking or because they had separated, reported less disturbance the longer the time that had elapsed.

Not surprisingly, the rate of marital breakdown is high when a serious drinking problem exists for one or other partner. Unrelieved stress, particularly compounded with hopelessness arising out of expectations for change being repeatedly dashed, is bound to lead to thoughts of terminating the marriage as a solution. Indeed many observers of alcoholism-complicated marriages have expressed surprise that so many such marriages survive at all. Survival of marriage is not so surprising, however, if one considers the many commonsense barriers against marital breakdown. Feelings of obligation to children, moral restraints, external pressure from relatives or the local community, legal difficulties, a wife's lack of independent source of income, and an absence of anyone to take the partner's place — these are amongst the many factors that clearly bear upon the decision to endure hardship or to escape from it.

The Impact on Children

It is now fairly well established that one group of people with a high risk of having serious drinking problems are people who themselves had a problem drinking parent. Great efforts have been made in recent years to involve husbands or wives of people with drinking problems in treatment and counselling programmes and in research, but the same efforts have not been made with regard to children. Presumably this is because all of us, the problem drinker, the spouse, the counsellor and the researcher, are anxious to protect the innocence of children who we feel may not have full knowledge of the problem or cannot understand it or could have little influence on it. This author's limited experience of this (Wilson & Orford, 1978) and that of others such as Cork (1969) suggest otherwise. When effort is made to overcome the inevitable barriers that exist in talking to children who are living with a problem drinking parent, they are frequently found not only to share many of the same problems with which we are more familiar in spouses of alcoholics, but also to have highly perceptive comments to make about the family and its problems and about their own reactions to it.

Firstly, most of the children interviewed in the Wilson and Orford study shared the non-drinking parent's uncertainty about what to make of the problem and how to react to it. In fact, it often seemed that the long-drawn-out process of realising that a problem existed, deciding what it is that is wrong, and putting a name to it, was sometimes made even more tortuous for a child on account of the conspiracy of silence which surrounded the problem. It is obviously no simple matter for parents to decide whether children should be put fully in the picture about the problem, but it is easy for parents to underestimate the knowledge and understanding that their children already possess.

When children are well informed about what is going on in their family, they may have a quite complex view of the matter, and as Cork discovered may put as much blame on matters other than the drinking, including the behaviour of the non-alcoholic parent. The latter may be blamed for provoking some of the problem, for keeping arguments going when they arise, or for not reacting firmly or consistently enough. A most interesting example of the last of these is given in Beverley Nichols's autobiography (1972) describing his experiences with an alcoholic father. He describes the build-up of his own murderous feelings of frustration during childhood as he witnessed his father's recurrent bouts of excess and his mother's continual self-effacement and resignation.

One aspect which is worrying, because it forms such a crucial component of child and adolescent development, concerns friendship formation. Cork emphasised this in her book and almost without exception the children talked to in the present author's research commented that they found it difficult to make friends for various reasons. Sometimes it was simply a matter of the parent with a drinking problem having a low tolerance for having other children around the place, but usually it was a more subtle matter to do with the child's unwillingness to enter a close friendship in which he or she would inevitably sooner or later want to invite a friend home. They often felt keenly that there was something abnormal about their own family and they had to know and trust a friend well before risking exposure.

Effects on Children

Are children adversely affected by these experiences? From the small amount of careful research that has been done, it does look as if children in this position are somewhat more likely to experience childhood problems and that these are more likely to be of the conduct or antisocial behaviour type than of the neurotic-anxious type — 'aggressive' problems rather than 'quiet' problems as one researcher has put it. Truancy, temper tantrums, destructive behaviour, hyperactivity, aggressive behaviour, and a bad reputation with their teachers are amongst the troubles which have been shown to be more frequent amongst children of problem drinking parents. Taking quite a different angle, one Scandinavian study found that children with a problem drinking parent were more likely than other chidren to be referred for specialist examination of physical complaints without any organic cause being discovered.

Although little is known of the long term effects, it can be stated with some confidence that a young man whose father has or had a drinking problem should be considered at high risk of developing such a problem himself, particularly if he has shown signs of deviant antisocial behaviour and is himself already a heavy drinker. Clearly we are talking here of only a proportion of young people, even amongst those with problem drinking parents. Nothing is known of other long term solutions or forms of personality development which are influenced by having had such a problem in the home as a child. Here again, as when discussing all aspects of this field, it is important not to generalise from a minority of visible cases. It is important to bear in mind that there are endless varieties of parental drinking problems, so that the nature of the stress is different from child to child.

What are the effects of drinking problems of differing types, levels of severity and duration? One factor which it seems may be an important indicator of the degree of severity of the parental problem, and possibly of its likely impact, is that of violence in the family. In one of the main studies of children's problems, the families were divided into those in which there had been any violence, and those without, and the rates of childhood problems were compared with control families without any parental drinking problem. Only in the first group, with a parental drinking problem coupled with family violence, was there a significantly higher frequency of childhood problems. Other research shows that wives use more coping strategies of all sorts when they experience violence from their husbands, are more likely to leave their husbands, and their husbands' problems are more likely to continue until they become chronic. Hence the violence may also be associated with worsening of the problem and the stress of family breakdown.

Because the concepts of 'alcoholism' and 'problem drinking' are so imprecise and cover such a variety of patterns and problems, and because children are so various, it is important that we try to be as objective as possible in this potentially very emotive field. Children vary in the age at which they are exposed to the stress of parental drinking, and in temperament. It is reasonable to expect quite different effects on different children, and even to find opposite effects in some cases. It is perhaps naive to suppose that all the long term effects need be negative. Parental drinking habits which create some problems, even serious ones, may possibly combine with other circumstances to strengthen the ego in certain ways.

Sex is a variable which is of obvious relevance. The speculation made earlier on the role of antisocial conduct in inter-generational transmission of drinking problems applies principally to men. With the recent increase in recognition of drinking problems amongst women, it becomes increasingly important to know whether similar or different mechanisms are at work. Part of the folklore on the subject is that daughters of alcoholics are very likely to marry men with drinking problems. No doubt this occurs, but much of the evidence is anecdotal and there is no research that indicates its frequency or indeed whether it occurs more frequently than would be expected by chance.

Before leaving this section, brief mention should be made of the possibility of foetal damage caused by heavy drinking during pregnancy. It has been claimed that this can lead to a recognisable syndrome in the newborn infant, the so-called foetal alcohol syndrome, characterised by facial and other physical abnormalities and a degree of mental handicap.

This possibility has received a lot of publicity, but it is of only recent discovery, and is still disputed. Although an expectant mother who is very dependent on alcohol and at risk of drinking excessively during pregnancy should be advised not to do so, there is nothing to suggest that this danger applies to more than a small proportion of the most severely alcoholic women.

The Family as an Interacting System

It has already been stated that the view of alcohol and the family expressed so far may be too simple. People involved in treatment or counselling often come to the view that other members of the family offer as much resistance to change as the problem drinking members themselves. Such a view is, of course, not confined to those who treat drinking problems, but is part of a general movement towards the view that the unit under consideration should be a marriage or a family as a whole. Part of this view is that it is artificial to consider a problem such as drinking to be located merely in one member of the family, or to view other family members only as victims of stress.

Early discussions of this possibility in the context of alcoholism were relatively crude case work observations influenced by analytic theory. For example, Whalen (1953) described four typical types of wives of alcoholics: Suffering Susan with masochistic needs gratified by marriage to a troublesome partner; Controlling Catherine whose needs to dominate, distrust and resent all men is similarly gratified by marriage to an incompetent and dependent male; Wavering Winifred who constantly leaves and then returns to her husband who is dependent on her; and Punitive Polly who behaves towards her husband like a scolding but indulgent mother.

Part of this view is that the mate choice process is far from accidental and that people sometimes choose problem partners knowingly or unknowingly in order to gratify certain needs of their own. Certainly in the study of 100 problem drinkers referred to earlier, as well as in other studies, it has been found that roughly half of the spouses, looking back, can see that the drinking problem already existed at the time of their marriage.

A further part of this perspective upon wives of alcoholics is that those who receive some personal gratification from the continued drinking of their husbands are particularly likely to break down themselves if and when their husbands cease to drink excessively. Again this suggestion is based largely on anecdote and it is hard to find more substantial evidence. Even if it did occur, other explanations are possible. One that has been proposed is that family members tend to break down in turns because there is not 'room' for more than one family member to be ill at a time. On this thinking one would expect a wife to 'save up' her breakdown until the stress that caused it was partially removed and her husband was functioning more adequately.

Person Perception Studies

There have been at least two types of investigation which have begun to come to terms with the complexity of the family with a drinking problem (or at least with the husband-wife pair) as a complex inter-acting system. One of these is in the tradition of person perception studies in psychology. In such studies each partner is asked to describe themselves and the partner, and possibly also to predict how the partner describes them. The results can be looked at directly, or after comparing two sets of descriptions (for example how the husband describes himself and how his wife describes him) to look for simil-arities and discrepancies. There have been several investigations of this kind of which that reported by Drewery and Rae (1969) is one of the most complete and best known.

The findings are complex and not always easy to interpret but a number of useful themes have emerged. One concerns male sex-role identity and dominance-dependence conflict in marriage. Most hus-bands, at least in Scotland where Drewery and Rae were working, describe themselves as high on needs for achievement, autonomy and dominance, and low on dependency needs. Their wives describe them in similar terms. This stereotype applied much less consistently in the marriages of men with drinking problems. The investigators interpreted their findings in terms of the husbands' confusion over their sex role and conflict over incompatible needs to be dependent on others and yet independent of them. They subsequently reported that these con-flicts were worse in a subgroup of marriages in which the wives also had conflicts in this area. Whether such conflicts over assertiveness and control predate the development of a drinking problem and partly cause it, or whether they arise in response to family role changes which come about as the problem develops, is another question. Whatever the answer, it appears that this area is likely to be an important one in understanding and intervening in family problems involving drinking.

A second aspect that has come to light in more than one of the person perception studies concerns simply the non-alcoholic wife's perception of her alcoholic husband. It is often maintained that such wives view their husbands as Jekyll and Hyde characters, loathsome when drinking but the opposite when sober. Certainly there are some wives who describe their drinking husbands in these terms but there is great variation and it certainly does not apply to all. Indeed there is a large subgroup who describe their husbands in quite undesirable terms when asked to describe them sober as well as when asked to describe them drinking. In the study of 100 couples it was shown that this was associated with other aspects of poor marital cohesion and that it indicated a bad outlook for the husband's drinking for the next few months. Such totally negative perceptions are a sign that the marriage is in a bad state and the prospects are poor both for the drinking problem and for the marriage unless they can be changed.

Observational Studies

The second type of procedure for investigating the family as a system is relatively recent, but although as yet it has involved only a handful of couples it is already producing illuminating information. Steinglass and colleagues (1977) have been to date solely responsible for this work. Their early work involved a father and son and also two pairs of brothers but their recent report concerns ten husband-wife pairs in which one partner (and in one case both partners) was a heavy problem drinker. The procedure involved a simultaneous hospital admission of both husband and wife for a few days, and drinking was encouraged and observed during this period. Observations and video taped recordings were fed back to clients. This is probably the first time that systematic and direct observations have been made of problem drinkers and their spouses during drinking. The general conclusions were that interactional behaviour became relatively restricted to a few stereotyped patterns during intoxication, that the quality of interactions was quite different during intoxication and during sobriety, and that couples found it very difficult to predict their behaviour during intoxication despite its stereotyped nature. The patterns are quite different from couple to couple. For example, Mr and Mrs B are described as normally polite and well controlled, with Mr B being the relatively more assertive and Mrs B quiet, passive and agreeable. Both were observed to drink heavily and to become mutually abusive in a repetitive fashion, with Mrs B in particular undergoing an apparent personality change. Mr and Mrs G on the other hand displayed a quite different pattern. Before drinking Mrs G was the more assertive, and Mr G talked only when spoken to and took on most of the housekeeping duties for the pair (living accommodation in the hospital was designed to simulate a home environment as closely as possible). They were awkward with one another and engaged one another little. With alcohol, on the other hand, the couple seemed more capable and comfortable while directly engaging one another, seemed more attentive to the other's feelings and needs and appeared more animated generally. Steinglass and his colleagues have speculated that alcohol may serve either as a sign or signal of stress within a family system which had previously managed without this coping mechanism, or might serve an important role in maintaining the equilibrium of the marriage or family as a system.

Although these early findings suggest that the effects of drinking on interaction may be quite different from family to family, there is a suggestion in this work also that conflicts over dominance and assertiveness may apply to many couples. The data shown in Table 8.1 are taken from the study of 100 couples to which reference has been made several times previously. Average values are shown for the whole group of 100. Taking the group as a whole husbands and wives are agreed that although drinking functioned to reduce the level of the husband's affectionate behaviour well below what was considered ideal (it was already somewhat low under sober conditions), it functioned also to increase the husband's dominance from a lower-than-ideal sober level to a level much closer to the ideal.

Table 8.1: Average Values for Affection and Dominance Reported by 100 Excessive Drinkers and Their Wives — Ideals and Amounts Attributed to the Husbands when Sober and when Drinking

	Ideal behaviour	Husband when sober	Husband when drinking
AFFECTION			
Husband report	12.2	10.7	9.1
Wife report	11.8	10.3	6.6
DOMINANCE			
Husband report	12.0	10.0	11.8
Wife report	12.0	10.3	11.4

Once again the findings point towards the importance of dominance as a key issue in a marriage complicated by a drinking problem in the husband.

Coping with Drinking in the Family

For better or worse the majority of families with a drinking problem in their midst find their own ways of coping without any special guidance and often after a long process of trial and error. If the view is accepted that spouses and children of people with serious drinking problems are at high risk of present troubles, and in the case of the children of future disorders, then the provision of supportive counselling facilities and of accurate information about the nature of alcohol and problem drinking would seem to be the least that should be readily and easily available to such groups.

Advising on how to react to the drinking member of the family is quite another matter, and here it is probably fair to say we are largely in the dark. The 100 wives in the author's study were asked how they had coped before they came for help and their answers indicated a wide range of different behaviours. Many wives had done what wives in their position are often advised to do, and that is to look after themselves and to get on with what they have to do as if they were relatively little affected. This is not meant to be a selfish technique, but is usually advised to help the rest of the family survive relatively unscathed and eventually by making the problem drinker realise that he must make his own decisions it may help to bring him to his senses.

We really do not know whether such coping is in the best interests of the whole family or not. In any case there are probably shades of different styles in which such a strategy might be implemented and these may be more important than the overall strategy itself. From the study of 100, coping behaviours which could be grouped under this heading were associated with a relatively poor outcome for the husband's drinking over the forthcoming 12 months. On the whole, it was the coping behaviours which seemed to involve engagement with the husband, even if the engagement was a stormy one, which indicated the better prognosis, and coping behaviours which involved avoidance or disengagement which held the worst prognosis. Some of the most discriminating items were the following:

Good prognosis	Poor prognosis
Starting a row when he gets drunk	Telling him he must leave
Making him feel small or ridiculous in public	Feeling you could not face going home
Pouring some of his drink away	Refusing to share a bed with him
Drinking some of his drink yourself	Consulting about getting legal separation or divorce
Hitting him	Hiding valuables or possessions
Going out to fetch him home	Keeping the children out of his way
	Feeling too frightened to do anything

It is possible of course that the relationship between coping and prognosis is an artefact and that both are just a sign of the severity of the husband's problem, with wives responding with avoidance when the problem is the more severe and has the worst prognosis. On the other hand, it is probably the case that avoidance and withdrawal are generally bad signs in any family because they limit the opportunities for mutual pleasure and reinforcement. It would certainly be consistent with a behavioural approach to family therapy to counsel spouses to remain engaged with their problem drinking partners but to make their position quite clear about the acceptability of different forms of drinking behaviour.

Children of parents with a serious drinking problem have rarely been identified as a group with special needs at all. Nevertheless the argument that they constitute a special high risk group and therefore a target for innovative preventive strategies is a strong one. There is an organisation called Al-Ateen for the children of alcoholics. However, its evangelical approach based closely upon Alcoholics Anonymous is unlikely to appeal to more than a small minority of children, and serious thought should be given to our response to this group. Alcoholism treatment and counselling programmes should consider whether they might make special provision for the needs of children. One possibility would be to make use of the idea of companionship therapy, as used for example by Goodman (1972) in the USA, whereby problem children or children at risk are allocated a young adult companion who meets weekly or more often with the child over a period of several months or more.

If the supposed general trends towards an increasing prevalence of alcohol-related problems truly exist and if they continue, we shall undoubtedly be called upon to invent humane and effective responses to the problems created by alcohol in the family.

9 PREVENTION

Marcus Grant

General

It is not only in the area of alcoholism that there has recently occurred
a significant change of emphasis towards the encouragement of a
broadly-based preventive approach. This change of emphasis has been
taking place on a wide range of health and social issues (DHSS, 1976).
It represents a recognition that a response to socio-medical problems
which is based exclusively or even primarily upon treatment services
can never do more than attempt to reduce existing levels of suffering.
Treatment, by definition, can be effective only after the onset of the
condition. Whilst improvements in the quality of *post facto* responses
to, for example, alcohol problems are to be welcomed and encouraged,
it is clearly of pressing importance to introduce simultaneously an
approach which seeks to minimise the number of people experiencing
such problems and which seeks also to minimise the relative severity of
these problems. In human terms, advances in hepatology and gastro-
enterology are greatly needed, but so too are advances in whatever
strategies will prevent people drinking so much that their livers become
cirrhotic in the first place.

The concept of positive health as something more than just the
absence of disease is, therefore, at the root of this change of emphasis.
In preventing alcohol-related damage, the development of the individual's full potential is sought so that the use (or non-use) of alcohol is
seen within the context of psycho-social *and* socio-economic functioning as a whole. Inevitably, the precise target for particular preventive tactics may relate to the reduction of defined areas of damage, but
the overall strategy seeks to accomplish something which is, in effect,
larger than the sum of its parts.

Thus, particular preventive campaigns may have a variety of aims.
They may seek to reduce average per capita consumption or to convert
heavy drinkers into moderate drinkers. They may be concerned with
enabling people to cope with or eliminate dependence on alcohol. They
may concentrate on specific areas of physical, psychological or social
harm and seek to break the causal link between these areas of harm and
the excessive alcohol consumption which anteceded them. They may
even, though this is less common in the UK than in some other coun-

tries, promote abstinence from alcohol as a positive virtue which can benefit health. Not all these aims are, of course, strictly compatible and it is for this reason that it is important to understand from the outset that within the broad subject of prevention are subsumed many approaches. A comparison with the treatment field (which is described in Chapter 11) makes it clear that this is endemic to the subject, for in treatment, as in prevention, the broad ontological aim encompasses a wide variety of intermediate aims and an even wider variety of approaches to these aims.

Traditionally, prevention is divided into three kinds: primary, secondary and tertiary. The distinction is not always as neatly drawn as that numerical subdivision would suggest, but it holds true in general terms at least. Primary prevention is the business of stopping people ever getting into difficulties at all; it generally refers to health education campaigns directed towards the young and to certain aspects of fiscal and licensing controls. Secondary prevention is concerned with the early identification of incipient problems, both through screening mechanisms and through the application of education to particularly vulnerable groups, where the likelihood of high rates of alcohol problems is greater. Tertiary prevention has as its aim the motivation of those who are known to be damaging themselves towards accepting some form of appropriate treatment.

These three kinds of prevention can therefore be seen as forming a continuum which begins with wholly naive subjects and reaches well into what might be thought of as more legitimately the treatment area. Indeed, instead of thinking about prevention and treatment as somehow two rather separate activities, it should now be apparent that it is in fact the same continuum which can reach from the foetal alcohol syndrome to delirium tremens. There is no dividing line between prevention and treatment, except the reluctance (and, some would say, the competence) of the practitioners of the one to become involved in dealing with the other. Indeed, increasingly, treatment approaches are coming to rely upon what might once have been thought of as preventive education, while prevention is coming to include self-monitoring techniques borrowed from the treatment area.

Many different influences make their impact upon the way in which an individual develops particular patterns of drinking behaviour. Prevention is concerned, therefore, with the manipulation of these influences, whether singly or in combination, so as to encourage healthy drinking patterns and reduce the likelihood of alcohol-related damage. Given the three kinds of prevention outlined above, it is probably most convenient to review current theory and practice under two broad headings: firstly, societal controls and, secondly, education. Although these topics will be examined separately, it is important to make it clear here that the response of any particular society to the alcohol problems manifest in that society is likely to include items from both headings. Indeed, the evidence, such as it is, seems to indicate that the most successful way to deal with alcoholism is generally the most eclectic. By combining the best (best, that is, for the given situation, the most appropriate) of societal controls and the best of education, a pragmatic prevention strategy can be expected to emerge, even if, as is generally the case, it has never actually been conceptualised as a holistic working approach.

Societal Controls

In Chapter 5 of this book, Davies discusses the various operational definitions of alcoholism. The trend which emerges from his review of them is clearly that of a dimensional rather than a categorical model. That is to say, there is no distinct, predictable and categorically separate group of people known as alcoholics. Rather, drinking is spread along a single dimension and the extent to which people harm themselves and others depends in very general terms upon how much they drink. Other factors are also of obvious importance and individuals drinking identical quantities will not experience identical kinds or degrees of damage. The general applicability of this dimensional approach is, however, important to the consideration of societal controls, as is the discussion in Chapter 6 of the relationship between average per capita alcohol consumption and the prevalence of alcoholism.

The minutiae of the Ledermann hypothesis as expounded by de Lint and Schmidt have quite properly come under close scrutiny and this has resulted in some important modifications being required (Duffy, 1977). There certainly remains, however, sufficient evidence to support the view that taxation is a legitimate health education strategy in the area of alcohol consumption. Yarrow's seminal little paper (Semple & Yarrow, 1974) on the situation in Scotland emphasises this point particularly vividly. In the figure reproduced here, the consumption of whisky and its relative cost in the UK from 1950 to 1970 are shown and the changes are compared with the rate of admissions for alcoholism to Scottish hospitals since 1956 (reliable data being unavailable on this count for the period 1950-55).

It is difficult to ignore the similarity of the curves illustrating consumption and hospital admissions, as opposed to the converse curve

Figure 9.1: Whisky Consumption, Price, Admissions to Hospital for Alcoholism

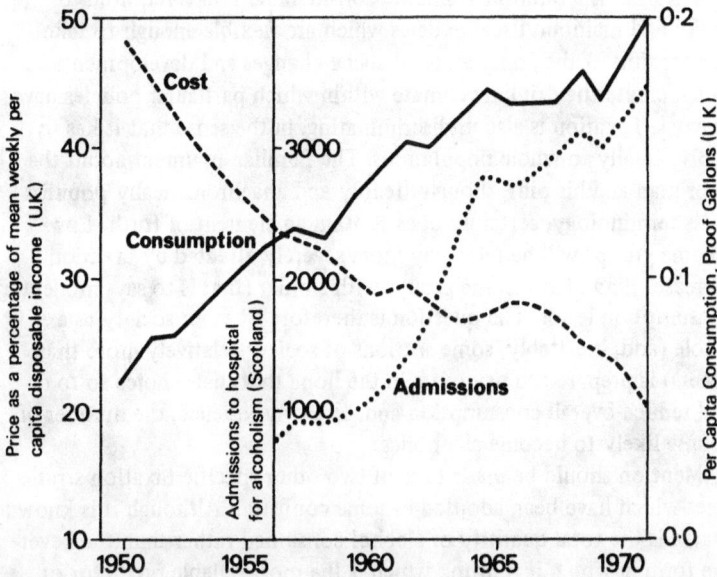

illustrating cost. Obviously, this is not a simple case of cause and effect. Many other factors will have influenced the situation. At the same time, however, it is clear that as the individual pays less for his bottle of whisky, so the total cost to society increases, in terms of alcoholism and the human suffering which accompanies it.

There is, certainly, a difficult tightrope to tread here. The argument, which has all the comforting appearances of common sense in the middle ground, becomes nonsense when pushed to either extreme. To ban alcohol or to increase taxation to prohibitive levels does not reduce human suffering in any real sense. It may (and even this is doubtful, given the increase in illicit production which would ensue, with no quality controls and thus with higher toxicity) reduce liver cirrhosis, but the increase in crime, black-marketeering and associated activities will more than compensate for any modest advances. In addition, all those who have been quietly using alcohol as a simple, cost-effective tranquilliser will start turning elsewhere for their self-medication, probably with far more damaging and costly (in health terms) consequences. On the other hand, it is clearly incumbent upon the authorities not to allow the *real* price of alcohol (taking into account, in this context, the

relative price of other retail products) to fall so far that general availability is increased.

Taxation is a blunt instrument. Considerable skill is required to
devise and maintain fiscal policies which are flexible enough to take
full account of the complexity of social changes and developments
which create the drinking climate within which particular policies have
to exist. Taxation is also undiscriminating, in the sense that it has to
apply equally to whole populations. The familiar argument about the
poor man and his pint, though drearily and anachronistically populist
in its terminology, certainly does contain an element of truth. Low-
income groups will be relatively more severely affected by taxation
increases than high income groups with similar (that is to say, moderate)
consumption levels. The question is therefore whether society as a
whole (and, inevitably, some sections of society relatively more than
others) is prepared to pay more in the hope that their choice so to do
will reduce overall consumption and, as a consequence, the number of
people likely to become alcoholics.

Mention should be made here of two other specific taxation strategies which have been adopted in some countries. Although it is known
that it is the total quantity of alcohol consumed rather than the beverage form in which it is drunk which is the most reliable predictor of
damage, it is nevertheless true that particular beverages may in particular circumstances account for disproportionate amounts of that
damage. This is particularly likely to be the case when, for whatever
reason, a product with relatively high alcohol content is nevertheless
relatively cheap. In such circumstances, a system of differential taxation may be appropriate, if only to restore that product to its proper
place in the alcohol hierarchy. Secondly, a more covert method of
introducing taxation changes is to hold price steady but alter the proof
level of the beverages. By this means, the real price of alcohol is being
increased but the cost of each commonly purchased measure of the
beverage remains unchanged. It has been argued that the alcohol-
dependent will still need to drink the quantity of ethanol to which he
has become addicted but it may certainly be the case that such a
strategy could have important preventive implications in reducing the
amount of the drug being consumed by those who regularly drink a
habitual number of measures such as three pints of beer a night. The
first of these strategies (differential taxation) was attempted recently in
the UK with regard to cider and the second (proof level reduction) has
been attempted in the USSR with regard to vodka.

Another major societal control is, of course, the permitted hours of sale of alcoholic beverages or, as they are often known, the licensing hours. The number and nature of licensed retail outlets, whether designed for consumption on or off the premises, together with the hours these establishments are allowed to remain open for sale and the classes of people who are allowed to purchase alcoholic beverages there; these are all factors which will influence the overall level of consumption in a particular community. It has, for instance, been argued that one reason for the difference in alcoholism rates between Scotland and England (it has been estimated that the rate is four times higher in Scotland) (SHEU, 1978) is the nature of the Scottish pub, which is still viewed as a machine for getting drunk in. Whilst it would obviously be simplistic to lay the whole blame for Scotland's alcohol problem upon the shoulders of the licensees, it may be that an improvement in the environmental ethos of Scottish public houses would have a beneficial effect. Further, the introduction of the continental cafe-pub has been suggested as a viable method of extending the range of beverage choice open to drinkers, as has the extension of the number and type of soft drinks.

Licensing hours as such are relatively manipulatable. They were introduced by Lloyd George under the Defence of the Realm Act when, during the First World War, the munitions workers were so drunk that arms were not reaching the troops at the front in sufficient quantities. Their effect was very dramatic, as is seen in Figure 9.2, which shows the relationship between consumption of spirits and beer, proceedings for drunkenness and alcoholic mortality for the years 1860 to 1935.

The most remarkable feature of this graph is the dramatic drop in all four rates which coincides with the period of the First World War. Clearly, many factors must have contributed to this phenomenon, not least of which was the absence of a large section of the young male drinking population, who were occupied in the trenches in Flanders. Nevertheless, there is a strong argument to support the notion that licensing laws represent the irreducible common element and it is worth noting that the Medical Statistician to the Registrar General's Department, commenting on the above figures (Wilson, 1940), said: 'All the indices available show the same feature of a sudden reduction on the outbreak of war, of which much the simplest and therefore the most acceptable explanation appears to be the increased difficulty from that time onwards of procuring alcohol.'

As in the case of taxation, there are obviously limits beyond which changes in licensing hours are likely to have counter-productive effects. It is a difficult area in which to evaluate the effectiveness of particular

Figure 9.2: Spirit & Beer Consumption per head (United Kingdom). Proceedings for Drunkenness per 10,000 (England & Wales). Alcoholic Mortality Rate per million (England & Wales). 1860-1935

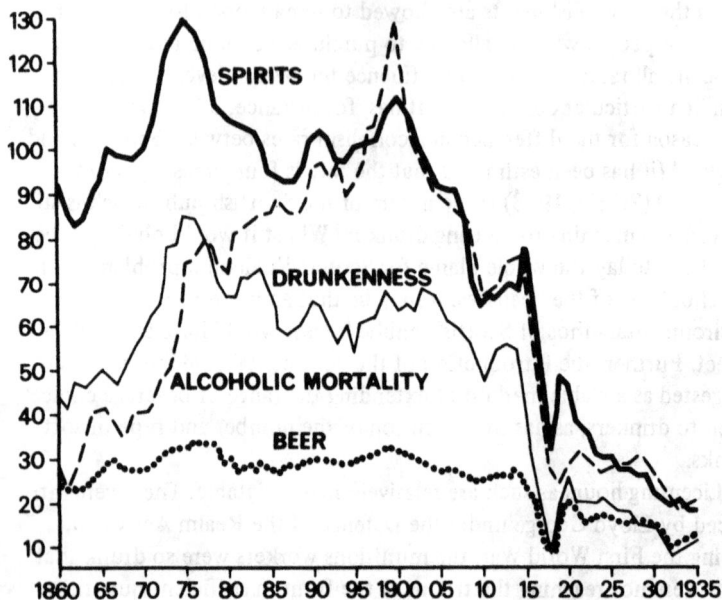

changes, especially when such changes are, as is often the case, relatively minor. Indeed, it is probably important to beware of falling easy prey to emotive and deceptive adjectives, such as 'civilised', where these are being used as the justification for particular courses of action. At the same time, what Clayson (1977) called 'the social pressure to drink' may well be a phenomenon which is susceptible to modification through the licensing hours and, at the time of writing this chapter, the effect of the 1977 changes in Scottish licensing would appear to bear out this hypothesis, though it is, of course, too early to reach firm conclusions.

The final societal control which will be discussed here concerns the regulations surrounding the advertising of alcoholic beverages. This is the area which tends to arouse the strongest feelings in the minds of the general public, or at least those members of the general public given to writing letters to newspapers and expressing opinions at lectures on alcoholism. Certainly, it is important that advertising should be strictly controlled so that excesses are avoided. The difficulty, as always, comes in defining excess. The UK Code of Advertising Standards seeks to ensure that young people are not made explicit marketing targets and that drinking is not associated with sexual or social success. On the other hand, myths of toughness, of maturity and of sociability have been associated with drinking since long before the advertisers started to weave campaigns around them. The balance between advertising which seeks to switch brand allegiance and advertising which seeks to maximise overall market potential has always been rather artificial and it must therefore be assumed that any given advertisement is working in both areas simultaneously. That being the case, it is proper that the public, and especially vulnerable sections of the public such as young people, should be protected from misleading advertising. At the same time, it should be noted that in those countries where alcohol advertising has been banned, no appreciable difference in rates of alcohol problems has been detected. There is a danger that advertising is seen as an appropriate target because of its accessibility and that this can lead to less obvious, but perhaps more effective, preventive strategies being ignored.

Education

Educating people about drinking and about alcoholism is very different from educating them about many other topics. Although they may well lack accurate knowledge, they invariably hold opinions about drinking and alcoholism, opinions which are often as firmly held as they are erroneous. Public health education about these subjects has, therefore, to assist in a preliminary process of unlearning before useful concepts are communicated. The process of unlearning can often prove quite troublesome, particularly if cherished views are being challenged. The other special problem about this kind of education is the gap between knowledge and behaviour. The aim of alcohol education is to alter behaviour so that disadvantageous patterns of drinking are avoided. Yet the target group for public health education campaigns is so wide that only broad approaches tend to be attempted. Even under the best of circumstances, the amount of knowledge which people retain is limited, the extent to which that knowledge is allowed to challenge existing attitudes is doubtful and the relationship between attitudes and subsequent behaviour is far from clear. It is, therefore, a difficult path which advice about drinking has to travel before it can be said to make any real impact.

Inevitably, health education has to be seen as a gradualist approach to alcohol problems. Significant changes are unlikely to occur within a few weeks or a few months. Years of coherent and planned health education may, however, be expected to yield results, particularly if specific aims have been identified from the outset and are adhered to throughout the campaigns. Parallels in other areas of health-related behaviour suggest that the timescale for achieving change has to be fairly extended. Spitting and smoking (both rather different from drinking though sharing some common elements) have both been influenced over a period of years by, amongst other things, broadly based programmes of preventive education. Thus, the positive results of any one poster, or newspaper advertisement, or television commercial may be very small indeed, but since the aim is to bring about an alteration in a deeply rooted social attitude and to modify a complex and significant piece of behaviour, it is by the accumulation of such small positive results that progress will be made.

Increasing attention is being paid of late to various self-monitoring techniques, based upon behavioural psychology, which can lead to a greater awareness of the way in which alcohol is used by an individual (Miller & Munoz, 1976). At present, the majority of the population is still, for example, far from clear about the relative strengths of different beverage types or the rate at which alcohol is oxidised in the body. Information on such subjects linked, as it can be, to drunken driving legislation, is likely to be seen as highly relevant by the population at large. An increased awareness of these issues can thus open the way to a more extensive form of self-monitoring whereby the whole pattern of drinking is examined with a view to ensuring that the individual's drinking habits are in his/her best interest. Self-monitoring of this kind, whilst acting to some extent as a screening mechanism with important implications for secondary prevention, can also, by reinforcing non-harmful drinking habits, have a positive role to play in primary prevention.

Often, however, preventive education is directed, not towards the whole population, but towards special groups within it. Such groups may be selected because they are particularly vulnerable to alcohol problems or because it is thought that they are particularly in need of alcohol education. Of the latter category, children and young people form the most obvious example. Indeed, much of the preventive education which takes place currently is concentrated towards this particular group. The researches of Jahoda (Jahoda & Crammond, 1972) in Strathclyde indicated that children are forming their attitudes to alcohol at a very early age and it has been argued that health education during the first few years of primary school would be more effective than the common practice of leaving it until the final years of senior school, when a child is likely already to have established the basis for a continuing pattern of drinking. Both Jahoda's study and that of Davies and Stacey (1972), who looked at teenagers in the same area, conclude with recommendations that greater attention be paid to the learning which goes on within the home. As yet, relatively few health education campaigns on drinking have sought to influence children's behaviour through parents or parents' drinking behaviour through a knowledge that children model themselves upon them. It is likely, however, as the work of O'Connor (1978) and of Hawker (1978) is used as the basis for planning future health education campaigns, that this area will be explored more fully. Already, the range of resource materials available for health educators to use with children and young people has become considerably more sophisticated as well as more extensive, so that it is no longer necessary to be forced into showing again and again the same dated and inappropriate film.

Specially vulnerable groups within the population may be identified in a variety of ways. There are, for example, geographical areas where alcohol problems are known to be more common. If, therefore (as is always the case), financial resources are scarce, it may be reasonable to concentrate upon such areas in the hope of making the greatest possible impact. Since there are, anyway, such important differences between regional drinking habits, educational campaigns based upon specific regional practices may well appear more vivid and have therefore a better chance of being acted upon by the audience.

Another way of identifying vulnerable sections of the population is by occupation. The role of occupation as a causative factor in alcoholism is discussed in Chapter 7. Where occupations are known to have high rates of alcohol problems, specific educational initiatives can be undertaken which are designed to meet the conditions relevant to those occupations. The growth in the number of organisations operating alcoholism policies and programmes is an encouraging step in this direction, since the very existence of publicly acknowledged alcoholism policies is itself of educational significance. Preventive programmes are also relevant where the risk to other people of accidents caused by drinking employees is particularly high. Pilots, drivers of public service vehicles, operators of dangerous equipment and members of the armed forces are just a few examples of groups for whom preventive education is likely to prove particularly valuable.

Another group which cannot be ignored is those who are already known to drink a great deal. Although it is still not possible to indicate a safe drinking level which will hold true for every individual, it is nevertheless now reasonable, as the result of accumulated research studies, to indicate how, if a daily limit of absolute alcohol is regularly exceeded, the chances of encountering problems are significantly increased. Most would accept that 15 cl per day represented such an upper limit and many would suggest that, erring on the side of moderation, 10 cl was a safer and less contentious figure to set. Certainly, education can be designed specifically for people who drink that amount or more and such education can be directed towards the aim of making them aware of their vulnerability and suggesting ways of reducing their intake to less hazardous levels. It is in cases such as these that the advantages of having a range of acceptable aims for preventive strategies become particularly apparent, since it is clear that few heavy drinkers (particularly if they would not acknowledge that they were experiencing any problems) would be prepared, for example, to do anything but scoff at the notion of abstinence.

There are other specially vulnerable groups, such as the children of alcoholics, the children of total abstainers, pregnant women and some ethnic minority groups. It is important to note here, however, the conclusions of Room (1977), whose international evidence makes it clear that very many people, in the course of their lives, move through periods of what he calls 'troubled drinking'. That being so, it follows that an individual's vulnerability to alcohol problems is not a fixed quotient, but something which can alter very dramatically, depending upon his life circumstances at any particular time. A variety of interdependent prevention approaches is therefore required, some being more relevant than others at particular times and in particular circumstances.

A final word is required here about what might be described as the agents of prevention. There are, of course, some professional groups, such as health educationalists and, to an extent, teachers, who can be seen as having a specific preventive role. It is important to realise, however, the vast potential which exists amongst those who might more traditionally think of themselves as treatment agents rather than prevention agents (Grant, 1977). It was argued earlier in this chapter that the distinction between treatment and prevention is false. It follows, therefore, that treatment agents may be well placed to offer the sort of information and advice which can just as easily be described as preventive education. This is particularly true of those practitioners who have general rather than specialist responsibilities. Obviously, therefore, social workers, health visitors, general practitioners and others all have ample opportunity to undertake simple and economical preventive work. It is known that patients with alcohol problems visit their doctors about three times as frequently as the average patient (Cartwright *et al.*, 1975). Yet the majority of alcohol problems are preventible in something like the same way that dental problems or sexually transmitted diseases are preventible. It is not necessary to stop eating or to stop making love in order to avoid such problems; it is simply necessary to have received relevant preventive education and to act upon it. Health and social workers are accustomed, in a variety of ways, to offering advice in many complex areas of their patients'/clients' lives. Drinking is one area, touching as it does so many other aspects of social functioning which, despite its urgency, is still largely ignored. There is no need for the professional worker to feel diffident about offering such advice. It is in fact an integral and cost-effective use of the scarcest resource of all — human skill, energy and understanding.

Conclusions

The change of emphasis described at the beginning of this chapter is already happening. More and more reliance is being placed upon preventive strategies (both societal controls and education) to make improvements where previous efforts have yielded little reward. It is at such a time that those engaged in preventive strategy formulation become pressingly aware that much of what they recommend is based still upon an expression of faith rather than upon objective scientific fact. Little rigorous evaluation of preventive campaigns has taken place and the relative weighting which should be given to different strategies is more a matter of artistic cunning than statistical analysis. One is reminded all too vividly of the fable of the emperor's new clothes. Much that is said in the name of prevention is arrant nonsense and vanishes upon even the most cursory examination. In assessing the work of particular preventive approaches, it is essential to remember both the great scope of the overall aim and the hard practicalities of each piece of strategy.

10 SERVICES FOR ALCOHOLICS

D.L. Davies

If the definition of alcoholism suggested in Chapter 5 is accepted, then the purpose of alcohol services becomes clear. One element will be the obviation of harm consequent on intermittent or continual alcohol usage, the other will deal with dependence similarly generated. In both areas, there will be the need not only to deal with such when encountered, but also to take steps to prevent them arising. This latter aspect will be the responsibility not only of the conventional alcohol services but also of public bodies (parliament, educational institutions and the like) which are not normally thought of in connection with alcoholism.

Harm

If one divides the areas of harm into medical (psychiatric and general) and social (to include occupational and economic) a similar breakdown of the services into broadly medical and social is achieved. Because there is often no sharp division between these aspects of harm, because more than one kind of harm is frequently present in the same sufferer (or his family) at any one time, or at different periods during his life, and because medical and social services are very closely linked organisationally, this division of services between medical and social should not be over-emphasised, but used simply to provide a descriptive framework.

The existing medical and social services satisfy a wide spectrum of medical and social disabilities. of which alcoholism is but one. Most of the general measures employed are equally helpful (whether the presenting harm is consequent on alcohol usage or not), so that alcoholics can and do avail themselves of such general services without needing to label themselves (or be labelled) as such. Help to restore liver function, to provide for the support of children or separated spouses, to find work or be re-trained for another job, to draw sick pay and other social benefits, is available to all who fulfil the necessary requirements, whether such need is linked to alcohol or not.

It is true that until fairly recently there was some prejudice against admitting alcoholics to psychiatric hospitals for treatment of their dependence. This reluctance was based partly on the expectation of poor response and on the special difficulties such management encountered. This was less of a problem than might have been expected, because many alcoholics resented their inclusion among the psychiatrically ill, and demanded special provision for themselves. Equally many hostels did, and some still do, refuse admission to alcoholics, much as they might bar epileptics.

It is as well to remember the breadth of general provision for alcoholics, when embarking on a description of specialist alcoholism services and it will be appreciated from what has already been said that it would be unwise to judge the services available to alcoholics merely on such special provision. In the psychiatric sphere, those suffering from from alcoholic psychoses have always been treated by the hospital services available for all the severely mentally ill, extending, of course, to outpatient and follow-up services. Equally, alcoholic liver disorders, or neurological disorders, have formed part of the medical services available from general hospitals in the same way. Before and after such hospital care, these patients have always been the responsibility of what is now called the primary health care team – the general practitioner with his practice nurse and possibly a social worker. Social workers, probation officers, and others working in courts and prisons, have also dealt with people whose misfortunes stem from drink. In addition to these recognised alcoholics, there is probably a very much greater work load on all the services mentioned above, generated by those who are not recognised as such.

Special Provision for Alcholics

Medical Services

Since the early 1960s, alcohol treatment units (ATUs) have been seen as the core of such provision. Each regional health authority has at least one ATU located in a psychiatric hospital and usually having 20-30 beds in each. The term beds is particularly appropriate since the emphasis until now has been on inpatient treatment, conforming fairly closely to an abstinence-orientated regime, and relying on group therapy and what is usually termed the Alcoholics Anonymous approach, even to linkage with local Alcoholics Anonymous groups. Frequently, the outpatient referring is done from distant clinics in the main centres of population, so that contact before and after admission tends to be difficult and lacking in continuity. The staff are usually members of the psychiatric hospitals who have become increasingly specialised in this work. In addition to medical and nursing staff, they include psychologists and social workers, these last, of course, now employed by the local Social Services Department. With the extrusion of private beds from the National Health Service, there has been increasing provision of beds for alcoholics in the private sector in recent years.

Entry to specialised alcohol treatment units is mainly through other medical services. The primary health care team (the general practitioner, nurse and social worker) will provide a point of initial contact for many alcoholics. Some individual teams do provide the whole range of necessary help. Not infrequently, however, they will refer on patients to a particular specialised medical agency, according to the more pressing need (e.g. medical complications, psychiatric illness or dependence). Sometimes referral may be to counselling agencies, especially where medical and psychiatric complications or substrates are minimally evident.

General psychiatric services, increasingly provided elsewhere than in the traditional psychiatric hospital, may well afford specialised services for the alcoholic, not only where the psychiatric complications or substrates are predominant, but also in more complicated cases where their resources of psychological and social worker expertise are needed to deal with the more severe aspects of dependency. General physicians, who may receive alcoholic referrals as such from the primary health care teams, will also receive physically ill patients in whom, at first, the underlying role of alcohol is not particularly evident. In both types of case, they are very likely to refer on these patients to other agencies for treatment of alcohol dependence, once the progress of the physical condition has been satisfactorily assured.

Social Services

Social services are less highly specialised in their provision for alcoholics, away from the ATUs. This is not surprising in view of the generic role in which the modern social worker is cast. Hostel provision for alcoholics has in the main been contracted out to voluntary organisations. Such hostels began to develop in a small way in the 1950s, and have received impetus from a policy decision of the Department of Health and Social Security to provide funding on special terms for acquiring houses for conversion to this end, though continuing maintenance costs fall on local authorities (DHSS, 1973).

These hostels vary a good deal in style and purpose. Some concentrate exclusively on homeless alcoholics, many of whom have been in prison, and for whom the Home Office accepts some financial responsibility for assistance after release. Others are less exclusive, and are prepared to admit alcoholics not so socially disabled, with perhaps more expectation of positive gains from their stay.

In some hostels the aim is merely containment, with perhaps frequent readmissions, while in others, there is a goal of rehabilitation to a more settled way of life, and in some the expectation is more or less complete recovery to independence from this kind of support. Some hostels see themselves as providing what might be called welfare, others positive help of a therapeutic kind, with rehabilitation as the stated goal. The ethos of most, if not all, such hostels is similar to that of the ATUs. The general rule is that drinking of any sort implies discharge from the hostel, nor are clients admitted unless there is some assurance that they are off all alcohol at the time of admission.

Another important part of the voluntary sector is the increasing provision of counselling services from what are called information centres. Whilst information as such is available to those seeking it, the provision of regular counselling designed to help the alcoholic and his family (much as marriage guidance is given in other circumstances), is seen as an important service.

Some counsellors are paid, the source of such remuneration being from local organisations (often Councils on Alcoholism), which draw their funds from local authority contributions and donations from private (including industrial) sources. Many of these Councils are affiliated to the National Council on Alcoholism (in England and Wales) which also receives Department of Health and Social Security support in addition to the kind of donations already mentioned, and is able to offer some support for the counselling services mentioned.

Alcoholics Anonymous is the biggest self-help group in the voluntary sector. It is a fellowship of recovering alcoholics, with a religious basis and an appeal to faith, which operates around group meetings, and has elaborated a set of beliefs on the cause, course and outcome of alcoholism, in keeping with its own origins and orientations. In its 'twelve stepping' it also offers what might be regarded as a personal rescue and counselling service.

Prison services are available for alcoholics in some places, mostly following the traditional approach of the hostels. Some charitable and religious bodies should also be mentioned (e.g. the Salvation Army and the Church Army).

Detoxification Services

It is often necessary, before the treatment of the harm or the dependence of alcoholism can be initiated, for the alcoholic to be rendered free of the effects of alcohol, at least for an initial period. This has tradi-

tionally been done at home, by his wife, or (under less loving super-
vision) in the barrack-room or the prison cell, in a lodging house, or in a
ditch. Bearing in mind the potential for dangerous medical complications in this procedure, it is remarkable how relatively safe and effective
such regimes have been.

Where the daily intake of alcohol is so spaced as not to interfere
noticeably with work, the problem will still arise if the man is unable to
alter his drinking pattern, try as he will. This kind of withdrawal from
alcohol carries a more evident risk of medical complications such as
delirium tremens (see Chapter 2).

ATUs will tend not to receive drunks, but do, of course, admit the
drinking alcoholic, sometimes to a special ward for withdrawal of
alcohol, sometimes directing him through a general hospital facility,
from whom they would anyway receive patients first presenting there.

It is really the repeatedly drunken alcoholic, often the homeless
man, who does not fit into the traditional service pattern for alcohol
withdrawal, and special provision for these was initiated in 1977. Two
detoxification centres were set up, one being based on the 'wet hostel'
model, the other more medically oriented and situated within a hospital. In both centres, the alcoholic is received (usually from the police)
in a drunken state and is helped through withdrawal.

The Nature of Provision

The weight of existing special services is on institutional provision,
either in hospital or hostel. Both these elements are directed mainly to
the harm caused by drink. If one includes some hospital and now a
little hostel provision for withdrawing alcoholics from alcohol, it would
still seem evident that little of what is provided is directly related to the
dependency aspect of alcoholism.

Yet the real load of treatment in alcoholism falls on those who
struggle with the alcoholic's dependency. Most of the harm he does to
himself and to others, can, as a rule, be arrested and probably reversed,
in days or weeks, which is the time span of his stay in these
institutions.

His need for help to overcome his dependency, however, is to be
measured in months, or even years. Mere length of residence in an
institution, where he is kept away from drink, does not by itself seem
to do very much for his dependency, as witnessed by experience of
alcoholics leaving prison after long sentences.

Even allowing for some outpatient services from ATUs, and some
tenuous follow-up contact from hostels, little is available at present to

help the alcoholic combat his dependency. Insofar as he does get help directed to this end extramurally, it would seem to rest on group therapy, based, if on anything at all, on the view that he has a constitutional weakness, which is susceptible to modification by such means, and that such therapy will equip him to withstand the temptation to abuse alcohol once he returns to everyday life. Both approaches are being actively questioned at the present time.

If there were general acceptance of some alternative view of alcoholism, perhaps as a response to environmental pressure to drink, or the outcome of a lifestyle which encourages high quantity/frequency intake of alcohol, then present provisions would measure up barely at all to what is required. Altering lifestyle, unlearning habits, developing an understanding of how drink has harmed a man, are clearly best achieved whilst the alcoholic is out and about his daily life. These adjustments can be made effectively only in a dynamic situation, where the alcoholic can apply the principles learned to his own particular way of life. Occupational, domestic and social adjustments need to be made gradually and in line with each other. In other words, treatment of dependency must be largely extramural and sustained over a period of time. By these criteria, another look at the nature of present provision is long overdue.

Slender as is the special provision for helping established alcoholics, that for prevention is almost nonexistent. There is a statutory body, the Health Education Council, with a responsibility in this field, which exercises its functions though health education officers and in other ways. Health education is provided by education authorities as well as by health authorities, but it is fair to say that, until very recently, alcohol has featured relatively little in such teaching. No doubt general hygiene, dental hygiene, sex education, venereal disease, drug abuse, and many other problems have been seen to have priority, not least because there are plenty of accepted approaches which it would seem helpful to pursue with regard to all these, whilst the obscure nature of alcoholism as a 'disease' seemed to offer only a temperance approach to prevention. The current account of alcoholism in the manual used by teachers on which to base health education is, however, well in advance of previous statements, and reflects an enlightened awareness of much present day thinking in the alcoholism world.

Until recently, public campaigns, in line with those mounted against smoking, have been few, confined mainly to certain areas of the country and designed chiefly, it would seem, towards early recognition. If this has resulted in increased demands on existing services, then the likely gain in the long term is limited to what those services can offer over and above their earlier provision, and within the success rates below mentioned. If those further comments are valid, then there is little likelihood of the public health problem being solved simply by some increase in the number of remissions achieved, so long as such remissions comprise a few percent of the sufferers at large.

The Efficacy of Provision

Examined in terms of treatment success, there is general agreement that most programmes achieve a 55-70 per cent remission rate, if by remission one means having no further trouble arising from drink. Skid Row alcoholics have a remission rate of 10-20 per cent at the most and the question really does not arise with symptomatic alcoholics (Chapter 5). Whilst this may look satisfactory, it is really meaningless unless one can form some estimates of what proportion of alcoholics come to the services available to help them.

The total hospital and hostel special provision in terms of beds cannot be more than 1,000, which might afford help to 10,000 or 20,000 alcoholics at most each year, as against an estimated 500,000 individuals in England and Wales who have difficulties of one sort or another arising from their use of alcohol. It is therefore clear that only the surface of the problem is being dealt with. Even if one allows that some outpatient help is provided and that some voluntary organisations, like the Councils on Alcoholism, play their part, and even allowing for the self-help groups in the field, the position is not reassuring.

The other way to look at this problem is as a public health matter. Granted all the treatment provisions listed, the plain fact is that alcoholism has been increasing for the last quarter of a century at least, some putting the present rate of increase as high as 10 per cent per annum. Even if this is an over-estimate, it is indisputable that the present provision of services is failing to halt the tide. Bearing in mind that alcoholism is best regarded as drug dependency, it would seem unlikely that more provision of the present kind would prove any more effective in reversing the rising trend than provision of more chest units would do for lung cancer.

The Future of Services

There is general agreement at the present time that future provision of services simply by increasing what is now available is neither feasible, in terms of manpower and other resources, nor likely to be effective in reversing national alcoholism trends.

Hostel accommodation may well, with some increase, be adequate for what is possible to achieve with the most socially incapacitated alcoholics, but this group comprises perhaps 1 or 2 per cent of alcoholics and anyway has multiple social disadvantages, which would not necessarily disappear if they were free of alcoholism.

The ATUs have played a useful part in focusing attention on alcoholism and in providing opportunities for doctors, nurses and social workers to obtain more concentrated experience in dealing with such patients. These units have usually concentrated on one approach to alcoholism and its treatment, one goal and one method, so that those who did not fit into this have been sparsely catered for. Special units have worked under geographical difficulties, very often being sited away from the large urban areas from which their patients come, so that continuity of in and outpatient care has been difficult. They have not been used to any significant extent in a preventive role, nor have their staffs had the special educational and training opportunities which would have adequately fitted them for such. Because of current misconceptions, shared by those in a position to recognise and to refer, that alcoholics cannot be helped until they have landed themselves in very serious trouble, they have had little opportunity to help the most promising sufferers, those who have not progressed very far as yet along the harmful drinking road.

Yet a significant proportion of the case load of social work departments, of general practice, of general hospitals, of the probation and prison service, and of occupational health services, is provided by alcoholics, whether they are recognised for what they are or not. Since all the professionals in these and similar situations are giving time to these patients and clients, and since they all have the skills needed to help (medical and nursing skills for doctors and nurses, case work skills for the non-medical professionals), it would seem that a great army of professionals already exists which could, with some further training, learn to identify more alcoholic patients and clients. They would then be better placed to refer these on for special help, and some of the more difficult problems would call for this. It seems reasonable to expect that they could go on helping as they have done up to now, but *more effectively* because of such further training. This would seem even more likely to occur if they saw the likely form of effective help to reside not in quasi-religious conversion, nor in specialised psychotherapy, nor in drug regimes, but in the everyday application of the kind of sociological and psychological principles affecting learning and lifestyle of which they have already been taught something and could learn more. This argument has been further developed towards the end of Chapter 9.

Voluntary Counsellors

Though all such professionals exercise some health education functions in the course of their work with patients, clients and their families, certain groups have particular opportunities in this direction. Social workers, health visitors and others who see relatives and go into their homes come to mind, as well as occupational health nurses, who are specially placed to note the early signs of alcoholism in employment.

It can be argued that, with the extra skills needed for such work, even if acquired in courses which did not take up much time away from their work, no more time would be needed to afford skilled help as against what is now offered to the (largely unrecognised) alcoholic. Even if this is true, it might still mean that a great deal of time from highly skilled and busy professionals is unlikely to be forthcoming, or even necessary. Could it not be that others might be specially trained for such work, on a professional basis, or even on a largely voluntary one, as happens with marriage guidance?

Certainly there would seem to be nothing in what a service should offer to reverse alcohol *dependency*, which is where the greatest provision is called for, which is beyond the capacity of suitably chosen and trained counsellors to provide. The beginnings of such a service already exist. A few Councils on Alcoholism have developed well-organised services of this kind, which have filled the gap left by the statutory services in their areas for many years now (the Merseyside Council is the best example) and it is interesting to note in the case of that council that the help offered has mainly been along what one might call the educative lines mentioned above, with more than one goal of treatment. Elsewhere the National Council on Alcoholism has begun to recruit and train volunteers for service in information centres.

Future Services

There is much to be said for capitalising on the existing large pool of professionals in many fields, to whom already many alcoholics and their families present for help, whose time is already taken up with these clients or patients (whether they are recognised for what they are or not), and who already deploy medical, nursing and casework skills. With more education and training, at every stage of their career, these professionals could discharge their existing responsibilities to alcoholics more effectively, thus lessening the demand for specialist services.

Concurrently, these professionals would also act as agents of prevention provided that they fully understood the role of environmental factors in the development of excessive drinking. They would then be able to incorporate new knowledge into their existing work both in the treatment and prevention areas.

To support and encourage them, the service within which they operate would need a smaller group of more highly trained experts, specialising wholly or to a very great extent in this branch of work, and with the responsibility for advising their employing organisations at the highest level of the overall requirements of the service now, and in the future, in the light of national trends.

Among the first rank workers would be members of the primary health care team, social workers, health visitors, occupational health nurses, probation officers and others. Among the more specialised workers in the second rank would be existing staffs of ATUs, staffs of psychiatric units generally and a growing number of volunteers (whether paid or voluntary) specially trained to help their clients over the difficulties of overcoming dependency, largely by changes in lifestyle, whilst remaining with their families and at work. These two roles might involve the same professional at different times. Clients might be referred to the volunteer counsellors for initial assessment, and then be retained for counselling because the harm they show is best dealt with by a remedial approach to their dependency, or referred to, say, a medical agency, because their history suggests that they first need medical attention pending an attack on their dependency.

Clearly this kind of development in services, whilst economical on the time of existing personnel and achieving expansion, in part by recruitment of volunteers not as yet involved in the provision of medical or social services, will fail unless there is to be expansion of resources for the education and training of all concerned.

Whilst a great deal can be achieved by the development of existing facilities for such within all the professional groups concerned at all levels (pre- and post-qualification), there will remain a most important requirement for some specialised education, preferably multi-professional as well as multi-disciplinary, of a status which could only be ensured by locating it within a recognised centre of higher education, and providing an academic hallmark at the end.

The future shape of services as roughly outlined here would go some way to helping those in need at an earlier stage and on a greater scale than present services permit, without simply calling for more and more personnel of the kind at present employed. It would make some provision for prevention, which might prove effective through a gradual improvement in social attitudes to drinking. Even if such changes in public opinion cannot alone reverse or halt the increasing incidence of alcoholism, they might make more acceptable what measures of, say, a fiscal kind might be thought necessary for the public good at a later date.

11 TREATMENT APPROACHES

Paul Gwinner

Treatment approaches comprehend the clarification of treatment aims, the elucidation of goals, the development of therapeutic strategies and the establishment of treatment facilities. The nature of these approaches, therefore, is dictated by the described characteristics of the condition under consideration.

In the past two decades the orthodox view of alcoholism as a discrete, uniform, readily categorised condition of strong medical connotation has been radically revised. This former model, conceived in the temperance ambience and nurtured by the self-help group Alcoholics Anonymous and the medical profession, evoked treatment responses singular in aim and parochially clinical.

Traditionally all treatment approaches were pervasively contaminated by a singular therapeutic goal, that of total abstention. The alcoholic condition was conceptualised as an all or none state analogous to a bacterial infection; you either had it or you did not. The progression of this state was understood as inexorable, and aetiology considered to be invested in metabolic abnormality of uncertain but possible genetic influence. Uniformity of symptomatology was accepted and the patient population described as a homogeneous group whose alcoholism was explained in terms of predisposing personality defect or of biochemical abnormality rendering them allergic to alcohol. In truth this constitutional view of alcoholism is not supported by any strong scientific evidence (see Chapter 7).

The acceptance of this discrete or categorical model, as it is now widely described, implied a treatment approach of strong medical bias. This type of clinical approach, however, was only in reality suited to the management of terminal and somatic manifestations of alcoholism and to ephemeral contact with the alcoholic at the point of detoxification.

That the condition alcoholism could not be effectively managed, if this narrow medical model was adhered to, was reflected in the development in the late forties of community based self-help groups, of no medical connotation, by Alcoholics Anonymous. It is a historical irony that this organisation radically altered the treatment approach, but

intransigently retained the categorical and discrete model of alcoholism
— an irony that continues to affect the later development of appropriate treatment approaches.

Why it took so long for the conceptual shifts, which we are now
witnessing, to occur and the consequent changes in treatment approach
is unclear. In the slowness of these changes, the potency of conservative
temperance philosophy may be reflected. Retrospectively, however, it is
surprising that the discrete medical model should have been so long
persisted with, when it is experientially so patently inappropriate.

The emergence of new models of alcoholism interestingly occurred
after the description and elaboration of new treatment goals, rather
than, as might have been expected, acting as a precedent for them.

The first serious suggestion that there might be an alternative goal to
total abstention, that of moderate drinking, occurred in 1962 (Davies,
1962). Since that date the dialogue focusing on the acceptability of
controlled, normal, social or limited drinking as a treatment goal has
been expansive, ubiquitous, and unfortunately often sardonically
polarised. Recently the Rand Report, more correctly entitled *Alcoholism and Treatment* (Armor *et al.*, 1977), concluded that many who
did give up excessive drinking were later found to be drinking normally
and not abstaining totally. Rand and Davies do not stand in isolation
for the theme of controlled drinking has provoked a great deal of
research replicating findings earlier described (Lloyd *et al.*, 1975).

This elucidation of alternative treatment goals in alcoholism appears
to have provoked a re-examination of the orthodox medical model and
a subsequent new preoccupation with treatment approaches. A dimensional model of alcoholism with gradation of individual drinkers on a
broad continuum both in terms of consumption rates and manifestations of excessive drinking in social, psychological and physical parameters is now increasingly accepted. The adoption of such a model has
important implications in terms of therapeutic strategy.

The dimensional model permits and indeed encourages treatment
approaches early in an individual's drinking career and rejects the
therapeutic passivity inherent in Tiebout's formerly widely accepted
but misconceived 'rock bottom' paradigm (Tiebout, 1949). The incep-
tion of early treatment approaches allows interaction with those
drinkers who appear to be incubating alcoholism. It further attractively
draws preventive and treatment strategies closer together in a commonality of purpose which was formerly unadmitted.

A dimensional model assumes a gradation of drinking behaviour and
associated disability enabling treatment approaches to be developed

cognisant of the position of the affected individual on the drinking or disablement continuum. This dictates the need for goal setting both in terms of future drinking behaviour and in required changes on other behavioural parameters. Intensity of disablement may be a basis for negotiating treatment goals (Edwards, 1977).

Thus varied goals and flexible treatment strategies can be applied germane to the needs of the drinker, rather than the 'umbrella' approach evoked by the categorial model in which all pathological drinkers were grouped in a single goal modality, regardless of the severity of their problems.

Goal setting, in which the drinker should be actively participant, should focus not exclusively on drinking behaviour but should also embrace other behavioural parameters of possible aetiological or rein-forcing significance in the drinking pattern. The setting of a temporal constraint, in which the patient or client is offered a treatment contract for a specific period of time is preferred by some therapists. This stratagem is extrapolated from psychoanalytic theory but its applic-ability in the alcoholism field is uncertain as most drinkers appear to require an open-ended relationship.

The multifaceted and protean nature of alcoholism is now ubiquit-ously accepted. The consequences of pathological drinking, however, also impinge plurally so that the suitability of singular treatment approaches must be questioned. The responsibility for the implementa-tion of treatment approaches, therefore, should not be invested in a single discipline but in a broadly based team of professional and volun-tary helpers. The multi-disciplinary treatment approach fits the dimen-sional model of alcoholism comfortably. Unfortunately, although this conception is academically attractive, its implementation often proves difficult.

Multi-disciplinary treatment approaches demand a commonality of aim from workers of disparate skills, training, status and experience. Empirical observation suggests that although the multi-disciplinary approach is widely adulated it is only sporadically practised. Significant impediments to inter-professional communication apparently remain deeply entrenched at both political and personal levels.

Kalb and Propper (1976) have recently commented exhaustively on the synergism created between the professional and para-professional worker and its implication for treatment approaches. They describe the professional worker as adopting treatment approaches based on a scientific model of alcoholism in contrast with the para-professional who uses a craft model of organisation. The scientific approach is one they describe as based on inductive reasoning, rationality and freedom of investigation while the craft model uses skills gained primarily through direct observation and experience under the tutelage of a master craftsman, in this case a 'recovered alcoholic'. This latter model discourages critical analysis, and indeed the test of the craftsman's learning is his demonstrated ability consistently to replicate the performance of his teacher. Kalb and Propper pessimistically conclude that craft and scientific models cannot profitably co-exist as the dichotomy between them creates unique tensions and problems.

The implications of this paper are richly relevant to the present polarity which obscures the controlled drinking dialogue and also to the development of multi-disciplinary based treatment approaches which require co-operation between professional and para-professional workers. Many of the difficulties existing between such groups of workers appear to focus on emotive issues associated with differing professional orientation of workers, the mutual under-valuing of each other's professional contributions, and restricted professional training, all of which reflect status or professional insecurity (Rathod, 1977). It is likely that such impediments to communication will only be effectively overcome by early multi-disciplinary training of allied disciplines before chauvinistic attitudes have been experientially inculcated.

That such difficulties are intra-disciplinary as well as inter-disciplinary is reflect in a recent paper evocatively entitled 'The Reality of Medico-Psychiatric Co-operation' (Krasner, 1977) describing the fragmented approach to alcoholism within the medical profession. Clinical experience indicates that the different specialities comprising medical practice adopt a symptomatic treatment approach. This is exemplified by the surgeon or casualty officer who enthusiastically and competently treats the traumatic manifestations of the patient's excessive drinking but ignores the causative alcoholism. A holistic treatment approach within the medical profession is seldom adopted and many medical practitioners appear totally to abrogate the management of the alcoholic patient to their psychiatric colleagues. Joint clinics established between medical practitioners of different speciality as a specific treatment approach in alcoholism have been established only intermittently.

The shift of emphasis from the categorical to the dimensional model of alcoholism should have led to increasingly flexible treatment approaches in all treatment sectors. A wide range of treatment techniques of a psychodynamic, physical, behavioural and sociological nature are now available. The overwhelming impression, however, remains that treatment differences between agencies are often more semantic than real.

In residential agencies, either the hospital special unit or the hostel, the predominant ethos remains that of the modified or non-permissive therapeutic community. Many treatment agencies continue to employ pedestrian and poorly described group techniques as a primary treatment approach. The pervasive dominance of these eclectic group techniques, whose superiority as a treatment approach in alcoholism has never been satisfactorily demonstrated, remains unexplained. They are part of the rich folklore of alcoholism and appear to possess an internal dynamic provocative of unquestioning loyalty in both therapist and alcoholic.

Criteria employed for patient selection in group therapy are poorly described and promiscuously applied. Historically this may reflect the potency of the traditional Alcoholics Anonymous approach where no visible selection for inclusion in the group is operated.

The goals of group therapy vary significantly between treatment agencies, as do the interactive techniques employed and the length of time spent in therapy. The application of the dimensional model of alcoholism should potentiate the use of behavioural techniques as described in Chapter 12. In reality, however, comparatively few treatment agencies employ these techniques defensively conceptualising them as 'too sophisticated', 'research bound' or 'difficult to apply'. The use of these techniques does not appear to have significantly generalised from a few centres of excellence in which a psychologist interested in drinking behaviour is employed.

The use of educative programmes as part of a treatment approach is a comparatively recent development. Didactic educative programmes can be used as an initiatory treatment stratagem to induce therapeutic motivation and erode the drinker's pathogonomic defence mechanisms. Educative techniques can also be used as a central part of group or individual counselling to encourage the adoption of a new lifestyle. These techniques should not be confined to the drinker but also involve relatives and possibly professional colleagues.

It is experientially acknowledged that drinkers of stable pre-morbid personality whose dependence on alcohol reflects vulnerability to persistent social or professional pressures often respond satisfactorily to short educative programmes following enforced detoxification. An educative approach also characterises some of the counselling methods adopted by the community (Madden, 1975). A recurrent theme of treatment philosophy within the field of alcoholism is that of 'motivation'. The Rand Report returns to this theme when it states 'that perhaps the crucial ingredient in treatment success is not really treatment at all but rather the person's decision to seek treatment and to remain in treatment'. The factors motivating a drinker to seek help are not fully understood, are certainly plural and interactional in nature and vary significantly from drinker to drinker.

Coercion as a possible motivator has recently received renewed attention. The apparent success of coercive techniques in the industrial and military sectors has led some workers to suggest their wider application. Coercive connotations are inherent in the recommendations of the Blennerhassett Report on Drinking and Driving (Blennerhassett, 1976). This report recommends that driving licences should be withheld from the repeated offender and from those drivers arraigned with a blood alcohol in excess of 200 mg per cent until such time as they have received treatment for their alcoholism.

Coercive approaches may satisfy the demands of the authoritarian, but would remain difficult to implement even if accepted by society. Their assumed efficacy in military and industrial sectors may be attributable to the hierarchical organisational structure of those sectors, with their inherent ability to expel the alcoholic employee who resists coercion. Society as a whole does not possess such a capability and therefore extrapolation of coercive techniques from the particular to the general may not be practical.

The implications of coercion as a treatment motivator is moreover likely to increase the demand on treatment services already quantitatively inadequate. In addition, the application of coercive techniques to a condition of ambiguous definitional status is readily capable of abuse.

Conventionally, treatment approaches have been exclusively conceptualised in terms of the formal therapeutic interaction or relationship between the drinker and the professional or lay worker while the interactive importance of events peripheral or extraneous to these formal relationships has remained largely unrecognised. Drinking behaviour, it has been assumed, is an immutable phenomenon, accessible only to the formal treatment approach. This concept ignores the susceptibility of drinking behaviour to changes in the life events, psychic equilibrium and physical health of the drinker. This susceptibility is of possible explanatory importance in 'spontaneous remission' described by some workers as occurring in as high a rate as 50 per cent of alcoholics (Clare, 1977).

The potency of the informal treatment approach exemplified by the control exercised by a perceptive employer, concerned colleague or insightful relative is incapable of sophisticated evaluation but anecdotal evidence for its existence abounds, particularly in the early stages of an individual's drinking career.

Self monitoring, a now fashionable preventive strategy in some branches of general medicine, could be replicated with the alcoholic if the dangers of persistent alcohol abuse were more generally recognised. Individuals could be simply trained to monitor their own consumption rates, the extent of their temporal and financial involvement with drinking behaviour or the physiological danger signs of excessive drinking. The provision of alcometers by some publicans in licensed premises adjacent to motorways typifies this approach. A sophisticated type of self-monitoring is used in behaviour modification techniques which depend on the discrimination of blood alcohol levels by the drinker in a therapeutic attempt to modify the drinking response.

The development of specific treatment approaches suitable to the needs of particular groups of drinkers has received only scant attention in the past, possibly because of persisting beliefs that the alcoholic population could be homogeneously defined. Treatment approaches specific to particular professional groups have been described by workers in the military sector (Gwinner, 1976; Shuckit & Gunderson), while industrial treatment programmes are largely trade specific in client selection. The Medical Council on Alcoholism has developed an outpatient group in London specifically for medical practitioners which has never been described in the literature.

The recent increase in the numbers of young people seeking help with alcohol-related disabilities from treatment agencies has prompted the establishment of treatment settings specifically designed for the young. Young drinkers appear to experience considerable difficulty in identifying in conventional treatment settings which cater for a predominantly middle aged client. This has led to the development of both outpatient (Coyle & Fischer, 1977) and inpatient (Gwinner, 1977) treatment settings exclusive to the young drinker. Such programmes have not yet been fully evaluated.

Some workers have asserted the need for treatment facilities specific to the female drinker; such demands have doubtful clinical validity and are often politically rather than therapeutically based.

The relative effectiveness of different treatment approaches in alcoholism remains a contentious issue. The assessment of treatment outcome is further confused by the adoption of disparate criteria for success by varied treatment agencies, and inferior methodology in much evaluative research. In spite of these difficulties Clare has recently pub-

lished a succinct paper evocatively entitled 'How Good is Treatment?'
(Clare, 1977). In this paper Clare comprehensively examines a number
of important reviews of treatment outcome including those of Armor
and Stanbul, already alluded to, Costello (1973) and Emrick (1974,
1975). He concludes that few noteworthy differences among remission
rates for varied treatment methods have been reported and that regardless of type of treatment setting, remission rates appear uniform.
Additionally he comments that those studies that attempted to analyse
the outcome in minimally treated or untreated alcoholics suggested
surprisingly high rates of apparent spontaneous remission.

These conclusions provocatively challenge assumptions previously
central to traditional treatment philosophy and imply that highly
sophisticated, costly and lengthy hospital based treatment programmes
are no more effective than the low profile, unsophisticated and
economic community based programmes previously dismissed as facile.
Edwards and Orford (1977) have recently undertaken a study of two
comparative groups of male named alcoholics. The two comparative
groups, each of which totalled 50 randomly assigned alcoholics, entered
different management modalities. One group received a single advisory
interview and a subsequent monthly visit by one of the researchers to
assess progress. The second group entered a treatment programme
similar to that afforded by the conventional medically based treatment
facility with provision for both outpatient and inpatient approaches.

At review after one year there were no statistically significant differences between the two groups on a variety of parameters associated
with drinking behaviour. These parameters included drinking patterns,
social adjustment, subjective ratings of drinking problems and time
spent in hospital. These surprising findings prompt the researchers to
suggest that 'future treatment services should primarily be developed in
terms of economic and low key programmes. These would provide a
network of 'first aid' and counselling and a base for later planned
development when it is clarified what sort of service ought optimally
to be developed.' Suggested characteristics of such a basic programme
include a emphasis on comprehensive social, physical and psychiatric
assessment to avoid fragmentation of treatment approaches; the clear
definition with the patient and his or her family of the nature of the
problem and the careful setting of goals.

Inpatient care, traditionally the preferred treatment approach,
should be confined, it is suggested, to the management of severe withdrawal states, for life saving intervention and for the treatment of
underlying illness of a psychological or physical nature.

Treatment approaches in alcoholism are currently undergoing revision. In the past two decades traditional treatment approaches have been significantly challenged and their appropriateness further undermined by increased prevalence and incidence rates. The elucidation of more liberal goals of limited or controlled drinking has contributed to the erosion of orthodox views. The further involvement of the paraprofessional worker, with limited training as in the current voluntary alcoholism counsellors training scheme, has been encouraged, and the comparable effectiveness of the traditional inpatient approach undertaken in the special treatment units with a low profile watching brief community based programme seriously questioned.

Mansell Pattison, discussing models of alcoholism treatment, described the 'competitive monolithic' approach in which different facilities each offer their own brand of treatment as 'the' way to rehabilitation. They proclaim high success if the alcoholic follows their method and avoids the other programmes which are known to be ineffective (Pattison, 1973). The rejection of the polar and subjective approach is now essential if therapeutic gains are to emerge from recent modifications in treatment philosophy. It is a matter of concern that some of these modifications have induced a facile and unscientific response heavily contaminated with subjective prejudice associated with personal investment in contrary treatment philosophy of a type already alluded to in Kalb and Propper's earlier paper.

Further polarisation and competitiveness will only obscure whatever gains have been made in the convoluted ambience of treatment approaches. What is required is a period of reforming in which the plethora of new ideas are objectively evaluated. The methodological processes in the evaluative research of treatment settings require refining, while matching of treatment setting to individual drinker, the clarification of treatment goals and the examination of all the complex connotations of treatment motivation demand renewed evaluation.

12 BEHAVIOURAL PSYCHOTHERAPY

Ray J. Hodgson

The psychologist's global conceptual model of human behaviour, shown in Figure 12.1, is basically no different from that which is implicit in many other approaches and in essence the aim of behavioural psychotherapy (or behaviour therapy) like any other form of therapy, is to help an individual to change. It is only when we ask 'how can we best facilitate personal freedom from fears, compulsions and irrational beliefs?' that different approaches begin to emerge which emphasise different types of intervention.

The historical development of behavioural psychotherapy was linked to two related shifts in psychological thought. The first was a movement away from pure introspectionism followed closely by the growth of experimental psychology, 'the science of behaviour and experience'; the second was a belief that people must be viewed in their social contexts and that in order to understand and help a person to change, we must alter the focus of therapy and view the whole interacting system of the person, his actions and the environmental consequences of these actions. The person is still of central importance but the basic strategy of behavioural psychotherapy is not to produce change only through verbal explorations of intrapsychic processes (i.e. the mind) but to expand the locus of the intervention to include behaviour and the environment, especially the personal and social consequences of behaviour.

Figure 12.1: The System That Needs to be Changed

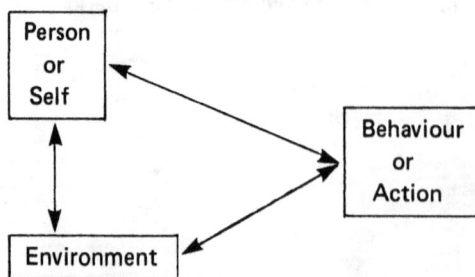

Two other principles have been enthusiastically preached and are now accepted as basic components of the behavioural approach. First, a behavioural analysis, as opposed to a psychoanalysis, is an attempt to understand the way in which the person, behaviour and environments interact as a system for the unique individual who is asking for help. Second, the behavioural psychotherapist should have a strong respect for the client's right to share in decisions about treatment, strategies and goals. This principle, of course, operates equally in other branches of psychotherapy.

Thoughts, beliefs, attitudes and expectancies must all be included in a behavioural assessment of a person's problems and nearly every psychological and behaviour therapy journal includes articles on self-control, mental rehearsal, cognitive restructuring and similar techniques which aim to help people change their habitual ways of thinking, perceiving and construing the world. The behavioural approach is not to ignore successful cognitive strategies but to recognise that the person can also be changed, and sometimes more easily, by first altering behaviour and restructuring environments.

A behavioural analysis is an attempt to describe the cues or cue complexes which influence drinking behaviour as well as the drinking pattern associated with these cues *and* the consequences of drinking in these different ways, including the various positive and negative subjective effects, e.g. elation, guilt and helplessness. In other words, what antecedent cues and reinforcing consequences make the alcoholic want to drink? The identification of antecedent cues must involve a global assessment of the individual's problems. Compulsive drinking has been associated with a large range of problems including the following:

helplessness and depression
failure or stresses at work
marital or sexual problems
build-up of tension or anxiety
phobic or obsessional problems
lack of assertiveness
social pressures from others
boredom and need for excitement
unemployment

These antecedents are usually explored by asking about those situations, thoughts and feelings which can lead to an increase in alcohol consumption or cause a relapse after a period of abstinence. Another set of cues must also be identified; these are the experiences which are caused by drinking and yet are cues for further drinking, e.g. feelings associated with intoxication, sobering up, withdrawal symptoms, minimal withdrawal symptoms and expected withdrawal symptoms. Treatment begins only when antecedent cues and reinforcing consequences have been identified, since treatment strategies usually focus upon modifying the antecedents and the consequences of drinking.

Reducing the Probability of Compulsive Drinking by Modifying Antecedent Cues

Compulsive drinking is defined as drinking to obtain gratification or achieve short term goals at the expense of other long term and more desirable goals which are considered to be more desirable by the drinker himself. Since any problem can lead to compulsive drinking, this section should actually cover the whole of behavioural psychotherapy, but instead I will deal only with the most relevant problems.

Follow-up studies have suggested that major reasons for relapse into heavy drinking are experiences of frustration, anger, anxiety, social stresses and social pressure to drink. It has also been demonstrated experimentally that alcoholics tend to drink more when subjected to interpersonal stress; consequently it is a reasonable assumption that learning to cope with these experiences would have a beneficial effect on the person and on drinking behaviour.

Progressive Relaxation Training (Bernstein & Borkovec, 1973) is a well-tested method of coping with anxiety. Clients are trained to lower their level of anxiety by relaxing various muscle groups, sometimes the calming effect being enhanced by recalling pleasant experiences. The relaxation skill is taught as a coping technique which can be used to prevent the escalation of anxiety in various threatening situations. Anxiety is not always 'free-floating' but is frequently conditioned to, and therefore elicited by, specific events and experiences so that relaxation training has an important part of play in *systematic desensitisation*, a method of reducing these conditioned anxiety responses. The client is first relaxed and asked to imagine a series of increasingly disturbing scenes which are associated with anxiety and avoidance behaviour (e.g. social situations), these imaginal exposures being followed by real-life practice where appropriate. The use of *biofeedback* to enhance muscle relaxation is a very promising and currently fashionable technique. By attaching two electrodes to a muscle group and measuring changes in electrical activity, muscle tension can be converted into a noise, the client's task being to reduce the pitch of this noise and hence reduce muscle tension; it is argued that learning the relaxation skill is easier when feedback is amplified and externalised in this way.

The basis of most behavioural approaches to *marital therapy* is to identify problem areas where relationships within the family have broken down and then to pinpoint specific changes in the behaviour of each spouse which would increase the other's pleasure and so strengthen the bond between them. Each person suggests a few changes in his/her spouse's behaviour and through negotiation a compromise solution is reached to which each member is then committed by a written contract. The new behaviours are listed in detail (e.g. listening attentively to wife without yawning); however, flexibility is maintained since the only criterion for a successful change is that it satisfies the spouse. Some of the satisfactions which are requested have to be worked towards very slowly if they are difficult to achieve, for example, tender caresses and changes in sexual behaviour. However, gradual changes in behaviour can lead to an increase in positive feelings and an increased probability of spontaneous, tender, affectionate interactions.

Feelings of social inadequacy of inability to express emotions can contribute to frustration and thus serve as potent drinking cues. Recently, methods have been developed to enable people to overcome such problems by increasing their social skills and especially their assertiveness. Typically, *social skills training* involves the identification of specific deficits followed by the repeated practice of graded tasks with the aim of gaining important skills. Sessions involve the role playing of person to person situations such as conversations, being firm with subordinates, job interviews, expressing affection to a loved one and expressing annoyance without being insulting. Feedback (sometimes videotaped) is given after each interaction and the therapist makes suggestions about eye contact, the content of communications, etc., usually emphasising positive feedback and encouraging every small improvement. Graded real-life assignments between treatment sessions are an essential component of these training methods.

The alcoholic often reports that not only does he lack a broad range of social skills, but that he does not have a ready answer when drink is offered in a number of situations. The finding that a large proportion of treated alcoholics give as their reason for relapse the social pressure exerted by others to get them to take a drink has stimulated a number of behaviour therapists to advocate that the alcoholic should be taught how to 'say no' effectively. One study used social skills training techniques to help alcoholics to cope with this specific situation. Actual incidents were recalled by each client in which social pressure to drink had been experienced and these were used in the role-playing sessions, e.g. 'You're at your brother's house. It's a special occasion and your whole family and several friends are there. Your brother asks you to have a beer.' Two psychologists role-played the client's social acquaintances (pushers) and used a variety of arguments in an attempt to coerce him to take a drink, e.g. 'What kind of a man are you who won't drink with his friends?' or 'One drink won't hurt you.' The alcoholic practised looking straight at the pusher, varying voice and facial expression where appropriate and confidently articulating appropriate replies. The evidence presented indicates that the alcoholics were able to modify their habitual way of responding to social pressure, and they reported increased feelings of confidence and self-esteem after successfully refusing drinks with their newly learned skills.

Since some alcoholics are unemployed, and furthermore have a feeling of helplessness about their job-finding abilities, the attention of counsellors must be directed to a very interesting report on a *job finding club* (Azrin *et al.*, 1975). Job finding was viewed as an activity requiring a number of complex skills which could be developed in a structured learning situation. The programme assisted the job seeker in every area that was believed to be influential in obtaining a job, emphasis being placed upon mutual asistance among job seekers, encouragement of family support, sharing job leads and role-playing of interviews and telephone conversations. Within two months, 90 per cent of the counselled job seekers (not necessarily alcoholics) had obtained employment, compared with 55 per cent of a control group; furthermore the average salary was one third higher for the counselled group.

Two trials have proved the value of marital, social and vocational counselling in treating alcoholic clients (Hunt & Azrin, 1973; Azrin, 1976).

This section has concentrated upon drinking cues which are the result of anxiety, vocational, marital and social problems. However, all other cues should be identified and, if possible, they should be avoided, at least during the initial stages of the treatment programme. These cues might be related to drinking friends, drinking situations and subjective feelings of boredom and sleep deprivation. The day-to-day planning of activities in order to avoid such cues is usually called *self-management*.

Even if the alcoholic can achieve some of his vocational, marital, social and personal goals, he may still experience a compulsion to drink excessively. Thus, each individual needs to develop his own 'fire drill', i.e. a detailed plan which can be put into operation when the compulsion to drink is experienced. Alcoholics Anonymous usually arrange for a friend in the neighbourhood to act as a counsellor in this type of emergency, whereas Mark and Linda Sobell teach a problem-solving approach (to be described later). As yet, we have no hard data to justify either of these strategies; nevertheless, the emergence of a compulsion to drink is such an important event that it is sensible to anticipate it, and even to discuss and anticipate relapses, so that various personalised coping strategies can be rehearsed.

Reducing the Probability of Compulsive Drinking by Modifying Consequences

Contingency Management is a term given to those procedures which help an individual to control his behaviour by altering the relationship between the behaviour and its consequences. Discovering the most relevant incentives for controlled drinking abstinence should be an important part of the ongoing assessment of the individual person. Treatment plans must be discussed in detail with the patient and he should perceive them as ways of helping himself rather than as ways in which the therapist or society exert a controlling influence; for example, the therapist might propose the following:

> You say that you don't want to let the hospital staff down, well how about this idea? Every time I see you, I'll take a breathalyser reading and we'll keep a graph for the next six months in Sister's office so that the nursing staff will be aware of your progress. You could also visit them every few weeks to look at the graph and discuss your progress with them.

Praise from others, or social reinforcement, is usually a very powerful incentive and should be used in an authentic but systematic way. For example, in one smoking study, 'Rapid Smoking' treatment was administered either by a cold detached therapist or by a therapist who encouraged and praised very small success. Three months after giving up smoking, 72 per cent of the praised group were still abstinent, compared with only 6 per cent of the unpraised controls.

When we start to tamper with the patient's rights, we are on to very dangerous ground and if, for example, social services are given only on condition that the alcoholic is sober then it must be just for a trial period, with his fully informed consent and only because he agrees that the strategy might be of some help to him. In one study ten chronic alcoholics who gave their informed consent were provided with goods and services through Skid Row community agencies contingent on their sobriety. Ten similar chronic alcoholics acted as a control group. The experimental group members had blood alcohol levels tested once every five days and only clients with blood alcohol levels of 10mg/100 ml or less were eligible for services and goods during the five day block; those above this level were denied them, as were subjects who were seen to be grossly intoxicated at any time during the five day period by agency employees or personnel. *Emergency services were never denied to any of the clients.* The control group received their services as usual, i.e. independent of their blood alcohol level. After two months the experimental group had achieved significant reductions in blood alcohol levels and arrests, and significant increases in hours of work per week. The control group showed no signficant changes on these measures during the two-month period. The study was conducted by Miller who concludes that 'wide scale use of this procedure on the basis of this report would be premature but replication of these results in a longer term evaluative study appears warranted.'

It has often been suggested that *aversion therapy* is another method of reducing the relative attractiveness of drinking compared to sobriety; however, the available evidence suggests that these procedures do not work and actually should not be used routinely.

Controlled Drinking as an Alternative to Abstinence

There are now approximately 100 articles in the scientific journals reporting that some people labelled 'alcoholics' can return to controlled drinking, although the evidence suggests that such a goal is more easily achieved by those who could be called less severely dependent. One study (Sobell & Sobell, 1976) of treatment directed towards a controlled drinking goal obtained particularly impressive results (Figure 12.2) and the specific techniques used by them are reproduced below.

1. The patients drank until quite intoxicated and then a few days later watched a videotaped replay. It was argued that the sight of their own mindless drunken behaviour would increase their motivation to avoid excessive drinking.

2. Subjects were given a failure experience in which they attempted to complete a series of tasks which were, in fact, impossible. Maladaptive responses to this experience were then analysed and better ways of coping were discussed. Successfully coping with failure experiences could eliminate one important reason for drinking excessively.

3. The next ten sessions were devoted to practising drinking in a controlled way. Drinking was allowed in a simulated bar and cocktail lounge and also in a simulated home environment. A large variety of

confiscated alcoholic beverages were supplied by the California State Alcoholic Control Board. The alcoholic's aim during these sessions was simply to control his drinking. It is known that the alcoholic tends to gulp rather than to sip his drink, so that he doesn't add a mixer but takes his drinks straight and that, of course, he drinks to excess. Consequently, in these controlled drinking sessions, the alcoholic knew that he would receive a one-second shock whenever he gulped, ordered a straight drink, made a second order within 20 minutes of his previous order, or exceeded three drinks in any one session. Actually, the maximum number of shocks received by any individual throughout the whole treatment period was six, and the majority of subjects received less than two. Most of the time drinking was completely controlled and the shocks were probably redundant. Furthermore, no subject found that he was compelled to leave hospital and go on a drinking binge.

4. A portion of each of the controlled drinking sessions was devoted to a discussion of the antecedent cues which would result in excessive drinking (e.g. an argument with the wife). A series of alternative ways of responding to these cues were then discussed and the consequences of each alternative were considered. In this way the alcoholic is trained to analyse the setting events or cues which influence his drinking and to work out an alternative way of coping. The Sobells consider this aspect of treatment to be of crucial importance. As an example they describe the way in which one alcoholic made use of this *problem solving technique* to deal with a strong desire to drink. He decided that he had a desire to drink because his brother was living in his house, sponging off him and attempting to seduce his wife. He then generated a number of possible responses to this situation, including moving from California to Chicago. After considering the long term consequences of each alternative, he decided to ask his brother to leave. To his amazement this was a perfect solution, and thereafter there was a distinct improvement in his marital relationship and a reduction in his desire to drink.

This multifaceted approach was very successful for alcoholics with a controlled drinking goal. Of course, the Sobells' approach embraces a large number of procedures and there is no way of knowing which ones are of crucial importance. The study demonstrated that a controlled drinking goal appears to be appropriate for some alcoholics, but it certainly cannot be claimed that controlled drinking is an appropriate goal for all alcoholics.

Conclusions

The behaviour therapy approach to the treatment of alcoholism is based

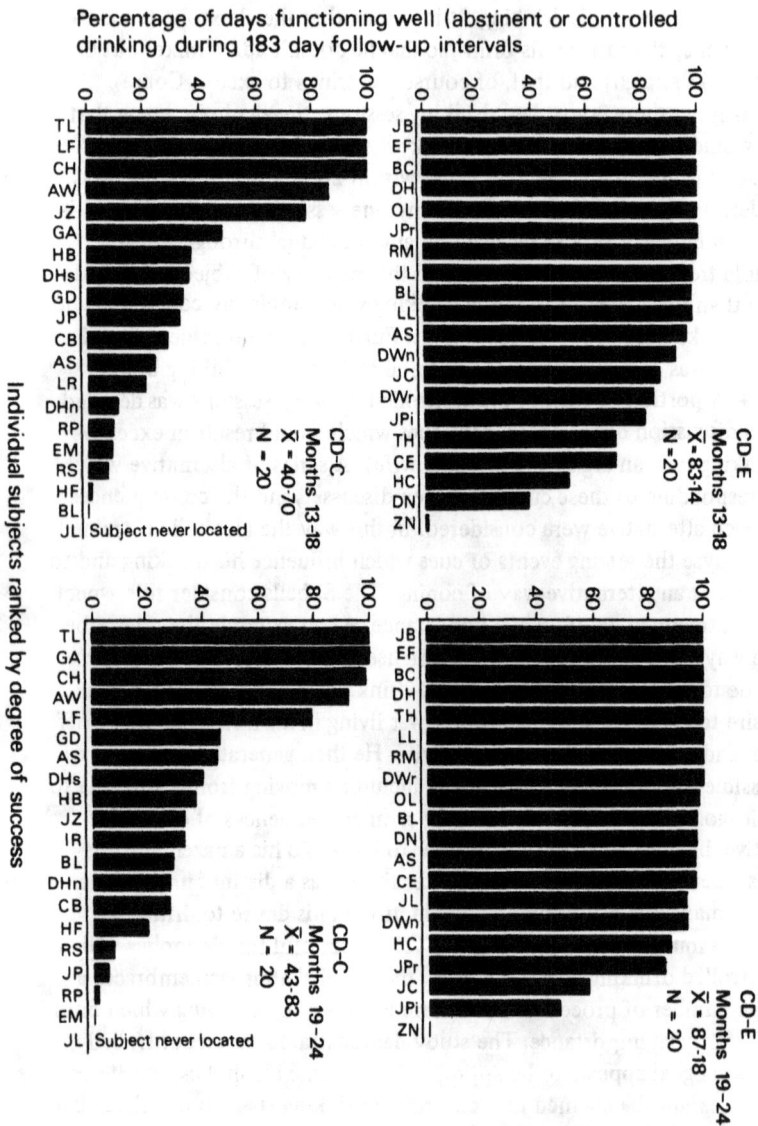

Figure 12.2: Results of Treatment Directed Towards a Controlled Drinking Goal

on the assumption that drinking is influenced by antecedent cues and reinforcing consequences. If an alcoholic nearly always drinks after an argument with his wife (antecedent cues) in order to relax or to forget (reinforcing consequences) then a social learning theory approach leads to the hypothesis that he will be helped if he can be taught alternative ways of coping with his marital problem and if sobriety (or controlled drinking) is made more rewarding than uncontrolled drinking.

The decision to drink or not to drink is based upon learned expectancies. We must ask what the alcoholic expects to happen under certain conditions (antecedent cues) if he drinks and if he does not drink. He will probably expect to feel anxious, frustrated or angry if he resists drink. His drinking decisions will be based upon these learned (often irrational) expectancies, as well as other factors such as his state of finance, availability of drink and expected feedback from family and friends. One result of successful treatment must be a modification of his expectancies especially as regards the negative consequences of resisting drink.

13 SOCIAL WORK THEORY AND PRACTICE

Linda Hunt and Judith Harwin

Introduction

Social work theory is of two kinds — broadly based general theory, and theory presenting a specific framework for practice. The first kind is particularly useful in clarifying the principles of social work practice (some of which are described and illustrated in Chapter 14, 'Working with Alcoholics'). Theorists are also developing a more 'precise, specific and consistent conceptualization of practice' (Roberts & Nee, 1972) which clarifies social work goals and the range of techniques and approaches associated with these goals. Both of these types of theory are are still being refined: as yet no one theory is complete and universally applicable. However, in the complex work of enabling people to make changes in their attitudes and behaviour, theory does provide useful ways of conceptualising the role of the worker (helper), of understanding the client's situation, and defining the skills and techniques most likely to help him. It is, therefore, surprising that little has been written about which theoretical frameworks have special relevance to work with alcoholics and their families. Social workers who have written about alcoholic clients have almost invariably concentrated on what is different or 'problematic' about alcoholism (Bailey, 1961), and thus have reinforced the general reluctance of social workers to consider that they may be able to help. Hollis (1964) has pointed out that there is frequently a gap between available knowledge about social and personal need, and the range of knowledge workers are actually using. This general comment has special relevance to work with alcoholics, for there is evidence of workers who have intellectual knowledge about social work methods and about the nature of alcoholism failing to integrate and use what they know (Cartwright *et al.*, 1975). This chapter aims to show how theoretical knowledge can be applied in work with alcoholics and their families.

Four issues crucial in social work practice will be examined through the concepts and frameworks of three theories which seem to have particular relevance (there is a body of social work theory derived from behavioural psychology, but this will not be discussed as its principal concepts and uses have been outlined in Chapter 12).

This approach will encourage a realistic appraisal of the help social

Table 13.1: Crucial Issues in Social Work Practice

The issues	The theories
The client's social situation	Systems theory
Assessing the client and his needs	Psycho-social theory
Establishing a relationship with the client	Crisis theory
Matching social work goals with worker behaviour	

workers can offer clients struggling with alcohol-related problems, and enable members of other helping professions to understand the relevance of social work theory to their own work.

The Client's Social Situation

Social workers consistently emphasise the importance of understanding the client's family and social environment, and systems theory probably provides the most help in considering the alcoholic client's environment (Davies, M., 1977). This theory perceives each of us holding membership of a series of overlapping and related social systems. An alcoholic client may, for example, be a member of one system containing his nuclear family, of a second containing his employer and work-mates, of a third containing the friends with whom he drinks, and of a fourth containing the court and probation officer with whom he is involved following a drunkenness offence. Although these systems overlap at times (e.g. the work system and the drinking system), the individual will have a different role and different relationships in each system (e.g. in one he may be father and husband, in a second foreman, in a third probationer). Some of these systems may be more difficult and confusing than others; in some the individual may feel valued and understood and in others rejected and criticised. If the worker takes time to understand the alcoholic's position in his complex network, he will begin to know in what areas his client needs help. For example, the alcoholic may gain most comfort from the system that contains his drinking partners, feel rejected in his family and criticised at work. In such a situation it is unlikely drinking can be reduced unless acceptance and understanding are increased at home and at work. These changes will often be possible only when the worker has direct contact with family members and colleagues at work and through education and exploration enables them to alter their approach to the alcoholic.

Systems theory points to a further and complicating dimension to the client's situation. The various systems of which the individual holds membership are contained within larger neighbourhood and societal systems. These systems, like the smaller ones, hold expectations about behaviour and attitudes to alcohol, and may impose sanctions on those who contravene these. For example, a neighbourhood which expects a mother to devote herself to the care of her children, and regards alcohol as a beverage associated with meal times, is likely to reject a woman whose children are poorly clad and left on their own for long periods, and who is known to drink alone in public houses. This woman may continue to contravene neighbourhood norms if she takes a worker's advice to become abstinent and consequently still experience rejection. The worker must be aware of these 'system norms' so that he can enable the client to live comfortably in her environment whilst remaining abstinent and find ways of working in the local community that will increase its capacity to accept out of the ordinary behaviour.

Systems theory not only helps identify the particular systems in which the client's primary problem lies, it shows that each member of that system interacts with (i.e. influences) every other. One member's behaviour is always to some extent a response to the way others behave; and other members' behaviour is to some extent a response to his. A change in one member's behaviour will affect everyone else and is likely to upset the habitual pattern of interaction, thus creating stress or malfunction. For example, the alcoholic father who gains control over his drinking will make major changes in his behaviour which will have important repercussions in his family. He may take a more active interest in his children, which they may experience as interference; he may spend more time at home and thus pressure his wife to adjust to a different pattern of activity.

A systems theory approach, then, keeps in the forefront of the worker's mind two important factors: (i) the alcoholic's attitudes and behaviour are an integral part of a well established pattern of interaction within his family, so the family will need to be involved in whatever counselling is undertaken; (ii) it is necessary to examine the client's total situation, and to estimate the significance of its parts (i.e. systems) to his drinking and his alcohol-related problems and to consider with which systems it is important to make contact. These factors form the basis for assessment of the client and his needs.

Assessing the Client and His Needs

It is generally agreed that a clear and precise assessment of the client and his situation is an essential prerequisite to effective 'helping'. Being effective in helping alcoholics and their families usually means enabling clients to make changes in their behaviour and attitudes. Theoretical frameworks for practice are based in a variety of perspectives on the origins of behaviour and attitudes, and suggest different methods of helping changes take place. Consequently each theory has its own approach to assessment, and each is useful as a method of helping some, not all, types of clients.

The systems theory framework was originally developed by research workers in the biological sciences, and later applied in the analysis of social phenomena. Relevant concepts of this theory have been introduced in the previous section.

Psycho-social theory is based largely on the conceptual framework of psychoanalytic psychiatry, and has developed through attempts to articulate clearly the experience of social work practitioners. It argues that effective social work treatment is dependent on the careful *study* and *diagnosis* of the client's strengths and difficulties, and emphasises the importance of preparing a detailed social history during the initial phase of contact with the client.

Crisis theory, which has its roots in ego psychology, perceives a state of crisis as containing the potential for personal growth. Crisis is 'a catalyst that disturbs old habits and evokes new responses . . . The challenge it provokes may bring forth new coping mechanisms which serve to strengthen the individual's adaptive capacity.' (Rapoport, 1965). A state of crisis is not regarded as an illness, but rather a situation in which the individual's present level or range of problem-solving skills is inadequate to help him return to a more balanced and comfortable state. The theory focuses on the client's current situation.

Table 13.2 outlines key aspects of assessment for the three theories chosen for their usefulness in working with alcoholic clients. The aim is to emphasise the differences in approach and clarify the reasons for these differences. (To make comparisons simple a family approach is assumed throughout. It should be remembered, however, that in some cases the worker will be focusing on other parts of the client's social network.)

Study of table 13.2 makes plain that the information contained in a referral to a helping agent, and the first few minutes of contact with a client are crucial for the basic material they provide and the judgements the helper makes about the methods and techniques to use. Three examples will help to clarify this point. The problem drinker in a state of panic at the point when he is facing failure at work, rejection at home, and a court appearance for debt is in a situation requiring urgent action, and is likely to respond to the crisis theory approach. A family

Table 13.2: Frameworks for Assessment

Theoretical framework	Psycho-social therapy	Crisis theory	Systems approach to family therapy
Rationale	Present difficulties are the current expression of problems arising from past experience	Crisis is a precipitant of change in the client and his family	Change is dependent on a readjustment in role expectations and behaviour
Aim of assessment process	To identify the strengths and weaknesses of the client and the significant others in his social situation	To identify the area on which help should focus through analysis of the current situation	To identify roles taken by individual family members, and to check these against role ideals held
Interview situation	Usually individual client and his most signfiicant relative seen separately	Client and significant relative may be seen separately or jointly	All the significant members of the family present together
Worker style	Eliciting information and feelings	Clarifying situation and identifying focus for help	Observing interaction and reflecting it back to the family
Focus	Early personal history and the development of relationship patterns	Client's account of the development and meaning of current crisis	Family roles and interaction in the here-and-now situation

made miserable by parental arguments, caused by different expectations of the roles of wife/mother and husband/father, and exacerbated by the husband's escape into excessive drinking and the wife's dependence on her children, is more likely to be helped by a systems orientated method of family therapy. A woman living a disorganised lonely life, longing for close relationships which she constantly fails to achieve, and attempting suicide in a state of alcohol intoxication, may need help based in the psycho-social method.

Establishing a Relationship with the Client

The central significance of establishing a purposeful and supportive relationship with the alcoholic is made clear in Chapter 14. Here the aim is to consider some of the necessary prerequisites for such a relationship, and to examine how theory can guide practice by focusing on relevant knowledge, skills and experience.

The level of motivation to work with the social worker has long been perceived to be crucial (Hollis, 1964). A high level of motivation has been associated with a greater likelihood of developing an appropriate working relationship, and this in turn has been associated with positive improvement in the client's situation. Crisis theory (developed by Rapoport and others (Parad, 1965)) gives emphasis to the significance of the social worker's level of motivation to work with the client. Both of these aspects of motivation are significant in work with alcoholics and their families, and are illustrated in Chapter 14.

Hollis states that it is essential for the client to be positively engaged in the helping process, and goes on to indicate that engagement will be dependent on the client's levels of motivation and resistance. (Resistance is described as being generated by anxiety, fearfulness and feelings of confusion.) Psycho-social therapy is particularly helpful in its consideration of resistance. It shows that a highly resistant client is unlikely to be able to engage in a purposeful relationship, even if he is motivated to do so. For an alcoholic resistance may be a consequence of anxiety about loss of competence and a fear of what will happen if his alcohol supply is cut off; for members of his family resistance may spring from confusion, anger and guilt about his behaviour. Hollis states that the components of resistance may be powerful influences on behaviour and attitudes even though the individual is not aware of feeling anxious or confused. In other words, the individual may have developed defensive mechanisms to protect himself from experiencing the force of these feelings. The client who shows a high level of resistance needs reassurance and support from the worker; when he is confident of support his need to resist will reduce, and his motivation emerge.

Ripple (1964) points out, 'Regardless of the specifics of goal and service sought or of the capacities available for use, it is the motivating pressure that provides the dynamic for engagement in problem solving and in using the help offered.' Motivation is largely dependent on the client feeling hopeful that the agency and the social worker will be helpful. Psycho-social theory suggests that clients who have not chosen to come, but have been sent to the social worker may have little hope of receiving help. This theory would suggest, for example, that alcoholics who have to report to the worker because they 'are on probation' or whose employers have arranged counselling sessions for them, are likely to be clients with little initial hope of receiving constructive help. In such a situation the worker would have to give special attention to raising a client's motivation to use the agency.

The significance of hope as an aspect of motivation is given detailed attention by Rapoport. She focuses on ways of working with clients who are experiencing an acute emergency in their lives, and so approriately emphasises the state of tension, confusion (even disintegration), and hopelessness that typifies an individual in crisis. She is clear that in this situation the worker must take direct action to increase hopefulness in the client, and identifies three things the social worker can do. First the worker can be active in his initial contact. This will mean using his 'authority of competence and expertness' (Rapoport, 1972) which may involve giving information and advice. For example the client who is drinking in the early morning because he has found this helps to control nausea and tremulousness, will be helped by information that shows this is escalating his problem and by advice on how to consult with his general practitioner so that he can be prescribed drugs to help deal with these symptoms of alcohol withdrawal. Secondly, in a state of acute anxiety and helplessness the client will be ready to put trust in the worker, who can capitalise on this by being positive and direct in his behaviour, and so achieve some immediate, real (if minor) improvement in the client's situation. The worker may, therefore, make the first contact with the general practitioner. Thirdly, and very importantly, the client will develop hope when the helping agent demonstrates (a) confidence in the method of work he is using and (b) commitment to his client. Social workers (and health visitors and general practitioners) seem typically to regard alcoholics as a hopeless cause, and to feel they have few skills or knowledge they can draw on to help them, so the two aspects of this third point are of particular relevance, especially as we know from social work practice that the workers' feelings spill into relationships with clients, and from research in psychotherapy how important to successful treatment is the therapist's commitment and enthusiasm (Malan, 1963; Truax & Wargo, 1966). Plainly attitudes of pessimism about alcoholics amongst workers, and feelings that theory is of little relevance, will colour relationships with clients so reinforcing the alcoholics' feelings of hopelessness, and reducing motivation to seek and use help. Points (a) and (b) will, therefore, be further elaborated.

(a) *Confidence in the Method of Work*

Confidence about method is often based entirely on the worker's intuitive sense of 'feeling right' about what he is doing. This aspect of confidence is important, but is not enough. There are now a number of theoretical models of social work practice which describe the behavioural science theory on which they are based (and therefore offer a rationale for practice) and then present a fairly precise analysis of goals and of techniques and behaviours the helper should use to achieve the goals. (Crisis theory is one such model.) If the worker is to be confident in his use of a method of work he must have a sound intellectual grasp of its rationale, its goals and its techniques and he must be able to differentiate it from other methods. He must also be skilful in his use of the specific techniques and behaviours the method demands, and know that there is a good fit between his method of helping and his client's situation and capacity.

(b) *Commitment to the Client*

This aspect of relationship is emphasised by all social work theorists, but is more fully explored in the psycho-social model. Hollis describes the social work relationship as being 'other centred', and this concept seems most useful in clarifying the idea of concern for and commitment to the client. The social worker's primary task is to engage in the relationship for the benefit of the client: he is charged to make sure he does not substitute his own needs for his client's, or impose his own prejudices and solutions. This has special relevance in work with alcoholics and their families as it is clear that workers tend to hold the ambivalence to drinking and the judgemental attitude to alcohol abusers still current in our society (see Chapter 3). If the worker is to help the alcoholic he must find ways of ensuring ambivalent feelings do not intrude into the relationship with his client. The psycho-social approach requires the worker to become self-aware about his negative and unhelpful feelings. It is argued that if self-awareness is achieved the worker will be able to put aside what is unhelpful and inappropriate and concentrate his attention on his client's feelings and perception, thus ensuring he draws conclusions and takes action appropriate to his client's needs. Implicit in the concept of 'other-centredness' is the principle that every client is an acceptable and worthwhile individual. The importance of this principle is demonstrated in Chapter 14, in for example the time, care and attention the interviewer gives Mr M. 'Other-centredness' contains two other important practice principles. It implies the client should have scope to make his own decisions and it highlights the need of the social worker to remain as objective as possible in his judgements and decisions. Objectivity is valued as a means of helping the worker towards a scientific, critical approach to assessing his client's needs and deciding what help it is appropriate to offer.

Crisis theory stresses that the client's level of hope and motivation to change will be increased if the social worker focuses on working *with* (rather than for) the client. This emphasis is of particular relevance for the recovering alcoholic who has a need for opportunities to begin to take responsibility for himself, and to learn new ways of coping with problem situations. It may, therefore, be most important in initial contact with the client to help re-establish in him a sense of autonomy.

The crisis model encourages the worker from the beginning to engage the client in clarifying the precise nature of his problems and in exploring methods of tackling those that are practicable. This does not imply the worker abdicating his role as expert, but rather that whilst using his expertise, he establishes a climate in which the client can require him to explain and justify what he is saying and doing, and in which the client is encouraged to influence and make decisions about the kind of help offered and the organisation of that help. The worker will achieve this by being open and direct in the way he relates to the client, by checking out that the client understands and agrees with decisions made, and by demonstrating his willingness to explain himself and to modify his views in response to the client's explanations and arguments. This will allow the social worker and client to challenge each other; and ensure negotiation and agreement between them about the focus of the work, the intervals between meetings, the order of priority of goals and so on.

This method of work may feel risky to workers accustomed to using a more passive or an indirect approach to clients. These workers may feel especially challenged by the freedom of clients to question the worker and by the shift in control of an interview that this brings. They may also be uncomfortable about challenging the client or about giving him direct feedback. It is important to keep in mind that crisis theory also emphasises that the worker's concern, commitment and acceptance provide the context in which challenge and negotiation can safely and purposefully take place.

Matching Goals and Worker Activity

The process of assessment leads to the articulation of the goals the worker seeks to achieve with a particular client in a particular social situation, and clarity about the method of work that will be employed. The helping agent is most likely to be successful in his work with his client if his behaviour is consistent, and congruent with both the goals and the method chosen. Chapter 12 explores this issue in relation to behaviour therapy and it is partly as a result of the work of psychologists using that method of treatment that social work theorists and practitioners have developed a better understanding of the importance and the difficulty of holding consistently to a particular theoretical framework and of using skills and activities that are congruent with the framework. A case example will help to emphasise the importance and relevance of engaging in this difficult area.

A social worker, experienced in working with alcoholics, was referred a family where the father, who had been diagnosed alcoholic, was a qualified social worker. The worker established that joint interviews with the married couple would be appropriate. In spite of this he began to work with the wife on her own, but was vaguely aware of avoiding contact with the husband. It was some time before he began to understand how judgemental and rejecting he was of the husband, and how threatening a client who was also a social worker could be. In this situation the worker had given the clients confusing double messages: he had presented a treatment plan, but followed up by substituting another and quite differently oriented approach which allowed him to act out his personal attitude to social workers who 'drink too much'. As he developed awareness of the way his own feelings were influencing his approach, the worker was able to change his behavioural style, and to work more consistently towards the goal originally established with the clients (i.e. to facilitate a change in the pattern of interaction within the marriage).

Three issues must be given attention to ensure that the social worker's activity is consistent and congruent. First, the worker must think through what the method of work he has chosen implies about the behaviour and techniques that it is appropriate to use. For example, a passive accepting style of behaviour, and the employment of techniques designed to encourage the client to explore his situation in an undirected way would not be appropriate for the client in crisis described on page 135. A systems oriented method of family therapy (with the second example on page 136) will require the social worker to use family interviews from the beginning and to be active in drawing family members' attention to their impact on each other. If the worker decided to use the psycho-social model for helping a family it would be appropriate to see the marriage partners individually and to collect historical data about each partner's early experience of family life, the expectations each has of marriage and so on: only later will it be appropriate to plan to introduce conjoint sessions (Family Discussion Bureau, 1962). When he is using this model the worker's behavioural style will have to be much less direct and active, and he will need to draw on his skills and techniques for encouraging the clients to freely explore the range of their feelings and attitudes.

It is, of course, easier to be clear about which techniques and styles are congruent with which treatment models when writing the chapter of a book than in actual face-to-face contact with a client. Each of us has personality traits and individual preferences that tend to influence the way we approach and relate to people. The second issue to which attention must be given, therefore, is the worker's awareness that his individual style may be disonant with the theoretical model he is using and the goals he has set. The worker may have to learn to emphasise different aspects of himself and his behaviour if he is to avoid giving his client confusing messages. This learning is difficult to achieve as it involves developing insight into one's behaviour and its impact on others. The quiet, diffident worker may well have difficulty learning how to be appropriately direct and active with some clients, and at the same time retain his quieter self so that he can use that as the basis for developing techniques that enable other clients to explore issues in a broad and reflective way.

Emphasis has been given in this chapter to establishing clear goals for worker and client. The third issue in matching goals and worker activity is concerned with ordering the priority of the goals established. The worker must clarify for himself which goal it is most urgent and appropriate to tackle. Although this is often difficult to do, it will help the worker to focus his work, and may also help to further clarify from what range methods of work he must choose. For example, in the third case example on page 136, the worker may conclude that the first goal must be to enable the woman to develop self-confidence and control. In this case the worker will provide regular contact in a one-to-one situation and will seek to demonstrate a consistent accepting and encouraging approach, whilst allowing the client a degree of dependence on the worker. Later, when the woman is more confident and less disorganised, the goal may become the development of skills in a range of social relationships and this may be achieved best through group work.

Conclusion

Social work theory has reached the point where it is possible to outline fundamental principles of practice and to classify the problem situations clients experience in ways which enable the articulation of goals and methods of work. This allows social workers, and other helping professions, to begin to identify specific areas of knowledge and particular conceptual frameworks which can be directly applied to work with people with alcohol-related problems.

14 WORKING WITH ALCOHOLICS

Judith Harwin and Linda Hunt

Introduction: Principles to Helping

Working with alcoholics involves three preliminary steps. The first one requires the worker to establish the contribution of alcohol to the person's difficulties. In the second the helper works with the client to secure his co-operation. These two processes pave the way for the third, in which an offer of help is made and a variety of strategies are examined to determine which might be most effective.

In practice all three steps create problems. They arise because the alcoholic often does not believe his drinking is problematic, or alternatively know it is, and denies it. This situation is aggravated by the problems which beset the helpers. They often have no working model of alcoholism which they can understand and use in their day to day work, and feel they lack the skills to put such knowledge as they have into practice (Cartwright *et al.*, 1975). The results of this are well known. Clients may express dissatisfaction with the help they are offered and workers complain they cannot persuade the client to accept the help they provide. It is common for confrontations to develop and the failure to reach agreement as to the nature of the problem may result in contact being broken off. All too often such mutually unrewarding contacts lead workers to decide that alcoholics cannot be helped and clients to conclude that no help is available.

This is paradoxical because whilst some areas of knowledge and skills *are* specific to work with alcoholics, the fundamental principles and procedures underlying help are essentially the same as for work with other client groups. They require the worker (a) to make an accurate assessment of the difficulties, (b) to establish a relationship conducive to their discussion, and (c) to select appropriate goals and methods to achieve them. The aim of this chapter is to examine each of these processes and the problems that they engender.

Assessing the Client's Difficulties

Establishing the Role of Drink

If the worker fails to establish the contribution of alcohol to the client's problem nexus he might find his attempts to help doomed to failure.

Why should this be so? Consider the following example: a father who is bringing up his children on his own comes to ask for help from the Social Services because he feels he can no longer cope. It emerges he has been drinking heavily to escape from his home situation. A common response might involve the attempt to alleviate the stress by mobilising various forms of social support. The worker might arrange day care for the children, provide a home help and hold regular supportive inter-views with the father to allow him to talk over his situation. In this type of approach there would be no specific attention to the excessive drinking in the belief that it would be brought back under control once the other tensions had been reduced.

This method is likely to fail for two crucial reasons. Firstly, the reasons for drinking are likely to change over time. Heavy drinking may become established as an independent pattern of behaviour, which itself is no longer brought about as a direct consequence of stress. The client may continue to drink at excessive levels because it has become a regular habit and is pleasurable in its own right, or alternatively because he has become tolerant to large quantities of alcohol. Secondly, the client who habitually uses alcohol to cope with stress, is likely to main-tain this pattern if further stress arises, unless he has been helped to realise the way in which he uses drink and has developed a strategy to modify his usage. For both these reasons an indirect approach to reducing excessive drinking is likely to fail.

This is not to suggest that attention to the client's drinking alone would be sufficient. But it argues that the helper must select drink as a legitimate focus in its own right, as well as responding to its conse-quences, in order to help the client solve his current problems and to prevent their recurrence. This will only be achieved if the role that drinking is playing in the client's problem is recognised from the outset. However, many factors militate against this.

Difficulties of Recognition

Helpers are often unaware that the commonest way for drinking problems to present is not in gross disturbances as manifest by delirium tremens or cirrhosis of the liver, but in a wide variety of social and medical difficulties, such as marital discord, debts, employment diffi-culties, gastritis and depression. Because of this, the worker is more likely to look for other explanations than to consider the possibility of an underlying drinking problem. To establish whether alcohol is impli-cated or not, the worker has to be aware of the consumption levels likely to be associated with the development of harm and to be competent in taking a drinking history. Often helpers find this difficult and express uncertainty not only as to the kinds of information required, but also as to the ways in which it may be accomplished.

This is reinforced by a tendency to perceive drinking as a taboo area with discussion legitimated only if the client raises the subject himself, or if the presenting problem is overtly drink-related. As these conditions rarely prevail, discussion of drinking is frequently neglected and the existence of an alcohol problem remains a matter for conjecture.

Recognition is as much a perceptual as a cognitive process. It demands that the worker not only knows that his client is drinking too much, but perceives this as a problem. Yet workers often disregard heavy drinking because they view it as evidence of a cultural norm rather than a manifestation of an individual problem. Partly this arises because in some departments, such as the Social Services and Probation and After-Care Service, the majority of clients derive from heavy drinking groups on whom the worker may base his own criteria of 'normal' and 'excessive' drinking. Partly it is a question of professional training and values, which, by stressing the importance of tolerance towards a diversity of subcultural patterns of behaviour, may actually deter the worker from discriminating between drinking which is culturally determined, but non-harmful, and that which is generating problems for the individual.

To emphasise the helper's difficulties in recognition is not to discount the part played by alcoholics. But it suggests that traditional explanations may have overemphasised the tendency of alcoholics to deny and hide their problems and failed to examine the contribution that helpers may make unwittingly to this situation. The remainder of this section will consider how these difficulties may be overcome.

The Process of Recognition

Three questions must be asked:

   (1) Is the client drinking enough to be harmed?
   (2) What is the harm?
   (3) Does the harm relate to the client's alcohol usage?

These questions are placed in a logical order. If the client only drinks occasionally or not at all the worker will not need to continue from question (1). If he is, then clearly the worker will need to gain answers to all three questions. It may take more than one interview to acquire the information but delay is likely to create more problems than it solves. Helpers often feel that it might be better to wait until 'the relationship feels right' only to find that this 'mystical jelling' does not occur and discussion may be precipitated by a crisis which catches the worker unprepared. How then can the worker put himself into a situation where he is able to initiate discussion around drink? Consider the following example.

Mr M., a forty-year-old milkman, was referred for a Social Enquiry Report following an assault charge. He had recently been divorced and his wife had been awarded custody of the three children aged fifteen, twelve and seven. The client was subject to a court injunction forbidding him access to the marital home. The offence had occurred when Mr M. had decided to go and see his ex-wife in the hope of persuading her to allow him back into the marital home. A fight on the doorstep ensued and the police were called in. The police report showed that there had been another episode in the past involving assault.

The first question which the helper must consider is whether drink could be a factor although it is not mentioned in the file. The evidence should arouse the suspicions of the worker because this type of offence is one which is commonly preceded by a drinking spree, and there is a previous history of similar offences. Of course, assaults of this nature may merely represent isolated episodes. To establish which explanation is correct, the worker needs to take a drinking history which will enable him to answer the three questions posed above. This can only be done when the client is sober, as otherwise he may give unreliable information and not remember the content of the discussion subsequently.

The interaction in the following sequence highlights the difficulty of broaching the subject of drinking *ab initio* when the presenting problem does not overtly relate to alcohol abuse and indeed may not be linked with it.

Interviewer Mr M., you've just told me you'd had a couple before you decided to go and visit your wife. How many do you . . .

Mr M. [interrupting] Oh, I always have a drink with the boys after work. See I start really early and finish round lunch. Then we all go down to the pub and have a pint together . . . [pauses] . . . Now hang on a moment . . . don't get me wrong . . . I only said a couple. I don't drink heavy except on special occasions, not just like that, not just for the sake of it. [angrily] You're not trying to tell me that a couple of pints is a crime?

Interviewer Well, no, I haven't said that at all. What I need to know is what you mean by a couple?

Mr M. Look, I'm no liar. I like my drink like most blokes I know. And if your wife were carrying on with another fella, I'd bet you'd want to sort her out pretty quick.

The interviewer cannot validate or refute his suspicions until he has definite information concerning the client's consumption and pattern of drinking. He therefore has to establish exactly what a 'pint' or a 'couple' means to the client. But Mr M. has clearly been angered by these questions and feels under attack. His answers are aggressive, possibly even evasive. This could indeed be a sign that he is hiding a drinking difficulty or could simply indicate that he cannot see the reasons for the questions and regards his drinking as a personal matter.

If the interviewer continued to focus on alcohol at this point he would almost certainly run the risk of provoking Mr M. into further hostility and denial. As the fundamental purpose of the recognition process is to enable the individual to receive help, it follows that the priority initially must be to create a climate conducive to the discussion of difficulties. This is most likely to be achieved if the worker can respond to the cues given by the client and use them to build up his understanding of the case rather than doggedly pursuing his own line of inquiry. In this way he will gain a much clearer understanding of the client's view of his situation which will be crucial in formulating help at a later date.

After discussing the issue of the alleged infidelity the worker then went on to explore further factors that led to the divorce by asking the client about his other grievances.

Interviewer Did your wife upset you in any other ways?

Mr M. She was always nagging me saying I didn't give her enough to pay the bills and that led to rows and sometimes I'd get a bit rough. Never beat her up bad, mind. But that nag, nag, nagging all the time drove me mad. Don't smoke, don't drink, don't waste our money. A real old killjoy. I'd ask her to come down the pub with me to get her out a bit. No chance. 'The pub's for drunks,' she'd say. So I'd finish up on my own.

Interviewer Can you remember what she alleged in the divorce petition? What did she say about you?

Mr M. Said I'd been cruel and that we just couldn't get on.

In contrast to his initial attempts the worker has now enough information to justify further inquiries into the client's alcohol usage.
Should he become antagonistic at this stage, the worker would be in a
position to point to possible indicators, such as financial difficulties,
quarrels and occasional violence, to lend support to his concern.

Interviewer Did she complain about your drinking?

Mr M. She never stopped. But that was her problem, not mine.

Interviewer But if you really didn't want the marriage to break
up it was yours too, wasn't it? What did she want you to do about
your drinking?

Mr M. She wanted me to cut down, because at that time I was
drinking heavy — 7 or 8 pints and then onto shorts. I'd a lot on my
mind.

Interviewer And did you?

Mr M. Wll I tried, but I couldn't just stop like that. The boys
would have had a good laugh. I couldn't say to them that the wife
doesn't like me drinking.

Interviewer If I asked her what led to the break-up would she say
it was the drink?

Mr M. It was the rows.

Interviewer But what were the rows about?

Mr M It was the drink, yes, it was the drink.

The interviewer has now succeeded in establishing a clear link
between drinking and the marital break-up. But of course it remains
uncertain whether Mr M. was still drinking heavily at the time of the
offence and whether alcohol had played any part in it. One might
expect that it would be relatively easy to establish this since the client
has already acknowledged the significance of drink in the past. Yet
people often find it much easier to admit to difficulties in their past
rather than current ones, because this implies that they have now
regained mastery of their situation. In the case of alcohol, the
difficulties are compounded by cultural factors in that an ability to
hold one's drink is closely bound up with notions of self-control. The
worker needs to take this into account and ensure that his client does
not feel too ashamed and degraded to be able to admit to a problem.
Nevertheless the worker must also be sure to establish the client's consumption in order to complete the recognition process.

Interviewer Well, Mr M. it looks as if drink has created quite a bit of trouble for you and your family in the past. Is that still the case? I mean are you still drinking 7 or 8 pints on one occasion with shorts?

Mr M. It depends . . . but now I'm on my own I get lonely and miss the wife and children. What else is there to do? I can't just sit in my room. Mind you, it's not every night. Just weekends and a couple of nights mid week, when I'm fed up.

Interviewer And what about the night of the offence?

Mr M. Well, I suppose I'd had a bit more than usual. I'd heard from my mate that my wife had taken up with someone new. I thought what it would do to the kids. And then you know the rest. But you're not trying to say I'm alcoholic, are you, 'cos anyone can go over the top once in a while?

Interviewer Perhaps you think that alcoholics are no-good down-and-outs and that's what makes you find it so difficult to talk about your drinking. But anyone can get into a situation where things get out of hand and they need a bit of help. I think you've been having a pretty miserable time of it lately and that things have come to a head. I think your drinking has been quite important in getting you into your present situation. You see, you've been drinking 7 to 8 pints at least three nights a week, plus shorts. Now that adds up to 35 pints apart from the spirits. That's the sort of drinking which we know gets people into trouble. Can you see that?

The worker has successfully completed the recognition process and established that alcohol has played a significant part in both the client's chronic marital difficulties and in his current crisis. Before he can hope to make an offer of help he has to ensure that the client shares his definition of the nature of the problem. Whilst this is by no means an automatic process, congruence between client and worker is vital to secure commitment. The next step must be to gain the client's co-operation.

Establishing a Relationship

Engaging the Client

The recognition process not only helps the worker to understand the situation; it should also serve to clarify matters for the client. This in itself is an important way of engaging the client. Equally important is the manner in which the discussion of drinking takes place. When clients seek help they have a dual problem; not only are they preoccupied about their situation but, during the interview, they are equally concerned to gauge the reactions of the helper. In this way the worker acts as a role model. If he is able to discuss drinking in an understanding way he can help open up a taboo area which can facilitate the acknowledgement of difficulties.

However, sometimes even though clients are aware that their drinking is out of control they still resist a change in their behaviour. Take the following case.

A married couple were referred to a social worker for help. Both were alcoholic and had received hospital treatment in the past. The wife had recently been dried out and had asked to see a social worker as she wanted a 'shoulder to cry on'. When the worker visited the couple they began discussing their drinking immediately, but said they did not want any help for it because they felt despairing about their situation and hopeless about the future. 'All that lay ahead was a coffin with no door.' The husband said that his liver was damaged and that if he didn't have much longer to live he'd rather go on being 'sociable' with his wife and share their usual bottle of scotch each night.

The worker came away feeling despondent. She concluded that the only options open to her were either to befriend the couple or to actually close the case. Significantly she rejected the possibility of trying to work with them on their drinking problem because of their apparent complete lack of motivation.

The social worker's reaction in such circumstances is not unusual. It highlights a central theme concerning work with alcoholics, which posits that they can only be helped if they are 'motivated' and 'accept' that they have a drinking problem (Sterne & Pitman, 1965). At one level such a philosophy is based on sound therapeutic principles: motivation is a well-known determinant of outcome, and its converse, 'resistance' is felt to be a major obstacle in therapy (as is further discussed in Chapter 13). But this view also has some disturbing implications for it suggests that the offer of help is conditional upon acceptance of the determination to alter behaviour.

Elsewhere, the literature on establishing relationships in the context of social work points out that 'acceptance' and 'motivation' are not all or none phenomena, but may be augmented or diminished (Ripple, 1964). It is also recognised that the early stages of a therapeutic relationship are particularly likely to promote ambivalence and denial of problems because the act of seeking help represents an admission of vulnerability and often generates fear that familiar patterns of behaviour may require to be changed. From this it is argued that the worker must help the client to articulate his ambivalence and conflicts as a means of promoting acceptance of problems (Bernstein *et al.*, 1974). By contrast much of the literature on alcoholism tends to regard motivation as an immutable attribute of the client. This is an important difference. In the former, motivation is perceived as an aspect of inter-action for which the worker must take some responsibility; in the latter view, responsibility lies primarily with the alcoholic. Because this renders the worker helpless it is likely to lead either to withdrawal or to confrontation tactics designed to force the client to see his situation clearly.

However, confrontation in the initial phase is more likely to produce a fight/flight reaction than acceptance because it ignores the conflict that alcohol represents to the client. He will often be aware that he ought to cut down or become abstinent: the reason he is seeking help is because he cannot do so on his own, and is therefore deriving some positive benefits from his use of alcohol. These may vary from the relief of early morning nausea to the conviction that life is drab and colourless without alcohol. If the worker focuses exclusively on the harmful aspects, he will prevent the client from expressing what he con-siders to be positive reasons for drinking and thereby debar the worker from understanding why the client needs help. So confrontation pre-vents the client from identifying the full range of his feelings and pre-vents the worker from understanding the client's subjective experience. Once the worker can appreciate the situation with all its contradictions and can communicate that comprehension to the client, he can help diminish the fear and anxiety which often underlie denial and evasion. He can then start to make suggestions as to how the client's situation might be improved and thus foster hope. Both these factors are vital in helping clients to acknowledge difficulties, for it is much easier to accept a problem if one believes it has some possibility of solution.

Thus contrary to popular belief the worker can play a very active part in helping a client to accept the existence of a drinking problem and thereby increase his motivation to work on it. It should be realised that the worker will succeed in this only when he actually believes that the client's life will be improved by altering the drinking behaviour. Often workers find themselves drawn into the client's despair and fear to alter his precarious equilibrium. This in turn derives from uncertainty as to the help which may be directed at the excessive drinking itself as well as to its consequences.

Setting Appropriate Goals

Setting Goals

'Of course I want my client to stop drinking only what can I put in its place?'

It is crucial to set goals in relation to the client's drinking as well as to its consequences if an overall improvement is to be achieved. In practice, most workers have little difficulty in making plans for dealing with the *consequences* of excessive drinking (Cartwright *et al.*, 1975). More problematic is the selection of drink-centred goals and the ways in which to integrate them into the overall helping strategy. However, if the role alcohol is playing in the client's problems has been clarified from the outset in the manner described, these difficulties should not arise. The worker will by now have a picture of the client's consumption level, its pattern and frequency and will also understand the precise way in which the client is vulnerable when he drinks. This information is vital to determine whether the client needs to become abstinent or to simply reduce his overall consumption or change his pattern of usage.

The decision for abstinence is generally taken when:

(1) There is evidence of physical dependence.
(2) There is evidence of severe physical damage, as for example to the the liver, or other vulnerable organs.
(3) The client has repeatedly tried unsuccessfully to control his intake.
(4) The difficulties ramify extensively through the client's life.

If the history of excessive drinking is short, or the problems appear confined to a single area of functioning, it may be worthwhile to consider advocating a reduction in comsumption.

Once the worker has made up his mind which goals are appropriate he then needs to gain the co-operation of the client to ensure his genuine commitment to the plans. This is often not easy and it is at this stage that the helper may find himself drawn into confrontation and hostility, as the client's initial impetus to seek help wanes with the growing pressure to make changes in his behaviour.

To illustrate some of the principles in setting goals and characteristic obstacles preventing their attainment, the story of Mr M charged with causing bodily harm to his wife from whom he is divorced is taken further. It will be remembered that the preliminary inquiries for the Social Enquiry Report had revealed that Mr M had a series of interlocking difficulties in which alcohol abuse played a part. The probation officer had therefore recommended to the court that Mr M. be made subject to a Probation Order and the court had accepted this recommendation.

Interviewer: So it really looks as if you're going to have to cut out drinking altogether for the time being.

Mr M: But, why, I'm all alone now that my wife has left me. I don't even see my children. I've got to have a little pleasure and a drink with the boys can't do any harm. I know lots of men who drink 7 to 8 pints a night.

Interviewer: I know there are many people who drink that much, but the point is, what happens to you? The last time, even though you'd had the injunction not to see your wife, you went back to her house and that's when all the trouble began.

Mr M: Yes, but it won't happen again. I was so frightened of going to prison and losing my job. I've learnt my lesson now.

Interviewer: Sitting here, that's all very easy, but what you're forgetting is how you feel and behave once you've had a couple. You start to feel resentful and remember that you ex-wife's taken up with another man, and then you want to go round and sort things out. As you said earlier, you don't really believe you and she are finished, do you? Once you've had that drink

Worker proposes an abstinence goal, but sets it for the *short-term* only, to increase the chances of it being attained. Client caught up in vicious circle whereby he drinks to relieve his misery, but does not understand that it only achieves this in the short term and subsequently intensifies the gloom (because alcohol is a cerebral depressant and not a stimulant). Interviewer points out the way alcohol causes problems for the client to try and help him see why he cannot drink with impunity, even though his work-mates are able to. Providing explanations helps reduce the risk of confrontation and in-creases the chance of gaining the client's co-operation. Client over-confident and unrealistic.

Worker continues to clarify the reasons for the abstinence goal with reference to the client's past and future. He uses a twofold strategy in which the client is helped to understand the drug effects of alcohol (i.e. by ex-plaining tolerance phenomenon) and to use this understanding to realise how he personally is affected when he drinks. The you believe it less and less, and you're sure you can get her back if you only try hard enough.

You've got to remember the way alcohol works. You told me previously that 2 pints doesn't really satisfy you. You need 7 or 8 before you feel any effect, because your body has become so used to large quantities that 2 pints is like a sip of water. Also, remember your past attempts to cut down. You promised your wife you'd stop, but didn't. Well this time you stand to lose the chance of seeing your children, because the courts aren't going to take a sympathetic view of someone who can't keep to his word and harasses his family. So for the present you've got to stop completely.

Mr M: But I can't stop whilst everything is so awful. My landlady says she'll kick me out if I don't pay the rent, and I've no money at all. If you can help me sort out those things first, I promise I'll stop.

Interviewer: I really think you need to come off alcohol first and then we'll start to look at your other troubles. You see, when people are drinking heavily, they just aren't as good at tackling problems as when they're sober. It's not to say you haven't a lot of worries but they may seem bigger precisely because you are drinking a lot. I know you're probably feeling drink is all you *have* got and it isn't easy for you. Once you're dried out, you'll feel healthier and your brain will

worker has to argue for his proposal and demonstrate his expertise. This is derived from knowledge of the clinical effects of alcohol abuse and from the capacity to relate these up accurately to the client's individual situation. Providing information is another important way of increasing commitment by promoting understanding.

Worker here provides a threat to increase the client's motivation, by pointing out the consequences of failing to stay sober.

Client puts pressure on worker to intervene before he commits himself to altering his situation.

Worker tackles drink-centred goals first before dealing with the harm. Although the two are interrelated the client is trapped in a downward spiral which can only be reversed when he becomes sober

The worker does not get drawn into 'rescue phantasy' but is understanding of the client's difficulties and undertakes to provide support. This is important in counter-balancing the threat used earlier.

be that much clearer. Then we can
start to try and sort out some of
your worries. That's why we'll need
to keep in close contact and at the
beginning I'd like to see you twice a
week.

It is important to note that the worker at this stage is only offering
his own resources. For instance, he is not mobilising social services to
make Mr M. less lonely; nor is he softening the situation by guaranteeing
that his client will definitely gain access to his children. His support at
this stage consists of showing his understanding and concern for his
client's situation and offering him the chance of frequent contact at a
particularly difficult time. Helpers often find this very hard. They are
used to 'giving', whether it is the dispensation of medication or the
provision of social resources. To actually 'take away' by removing the
prop from the person, would appear to contravene the fundamental
morality of the helping process.

It is for this reason that helpers often fall into the trap of colluding
with clients. Either they themselves try to find a substitute for the
alcohol *before* expecting the client to become sober, or alternatively
they allow him to continue drinking in the belief that it represents the
only satisfaction in his life. Both these approaches reflect the way in
which lay beliefs may interfere with professional therapeutic objectivity
by ignoring one crucial fact – that is alcohol is a source of harm to the
individual and the subjective benefits are likely to be substantially out-
weighed by the objective measures of harm.

Only one further point needs to be made. Had Mr M. still been living
with his family it would have been vital to set goals jointly to secure
their agreement, since the family exercise considerable influence on the
achievement of goals.

Achieving the Goals

Whilst it is possible to outline the principles and procedures underlying
the early phases of the helping process, the needs of the client become
much more individualised and specific once treatment gets under way.
It is likely that the worker will wish to draw upon a variety of stategies
such as family therapy, crisis intervention or behaviour modification
which will be suggested by the way the case has been formulated
initially. Some of those approaches were considered in some detail in
Chapter 13. However, there are certain problems which are likely to

arise and which transcend any specific mode of intervention.

Difficulties in Longer Term Work

Relapse

The post withdrawal phase is difficult. New problems may emerge for the first time; older ones may have to be faced either without alcohol altogether or with a considerably reduced intake. Whilst the client may feel physically healthier, this in itself can constitute a risk by making him doubt the validity of the initial formulation and encouraging him to chance drinking. All these factors make it unsurprising that relapse is so common. Yet it is frequently perceived as a sign of failure both by the client and worker and for this reason the topic is frequently avoided altogether. The worker may fear that he is indirectly encouraging his client to start drinking again if he mentions the possibility of relapse, or that he is subtly communicating an expectation of failure. He may also be afraid that the client will cease to believe in the helper's therapeutic expertise. Thus frequently relapse becomes an issue only when it occurs, and subsequent analysis of the situation takes place in an atmosphere of mutual disappointment and failure.

However, some of the sense of shame can be mitigated by anticipation of its possibility. It is important for the helper to indicate to his client whilst sober that he would wish him to maintain contact even if he were to relapse, and that they could use the experience as a learning episode by examining its reasons.

Limitations in Outcome

A successful resolution of a drinking problem does not automatically lead to improvement in associated areas of personal and social dysfunction. Whilst the client is drinking it is common for all difficulties to be ascribed to that fact. However, in some cases difficulties are incorrectly attributed to a drinking problem but in fact have *preceded its* development and accordingly persist afterwards. In other cases unhelpful patterns of behaviour may be learnt whilst the alcoholic is drinking and continue after control is regained because they have become deeply rooted patterns of behaviour. Consider the following case.

An alcoholic journalist, aged 38, had relapsed twice. His wife was a rather anxious person, who when her husband was sober, constantly asked him if he'd had a drink or felt like having one. Occasionally she persuaded their 15-year-old son to check up on his father by following

him when he went out. Her behaviour continued after her husband had
been abstinent for several months in spite of the fact that she realised
the strain it imposed on her spouse.

In this case the spouse was aware that her behaviour was counter-
productive but no longer trusted her husband and could not control her
anxieties.

Whilst the ability to modify attitudes and behaviour may provide
one limitation on outcome, the desire to make changes is another
equally important consideration. This is particularly likely to arise in
the context of the marital relationship. For example, the spouse may be
forced to take over areas of her husband's role within the family while
he is drinking, but be reluctant to relinquish these once he becomes
abstinent and is capable and interested in participating in family life
again.

For these reasons the goals must be open-ended and the worker
needs to constantly re-evaluate their relevance. These case illustrations
also emphasise that it is crucial to take account of the client's social
network because change in one person is likely to engender change in
others. Whilst this fact is well documented in social work literature (and
is further discussed in Chapter 13) the main thrust of work with alcoholics is commonly focused on the individual, with only minimal consideration given to the needs of others who are closely involved.

Keeping Open the Subject of Drink

Workers usually find it easiest to discuss the client's drinking whilst he
is in some form of crisis. Once this passes and the client regains control
of his situation helpers often feel less justified in maintaining discussion
around alcohol. There are several reasons for this. The sensitivity of the
subject is one important factor, which makes both worker and client
feel discussion is only legitimated when problems are rife, and, as a
corollary, that no language exists between them to discuss drinking in
the absence of urgent problems. Another explanation is that the worker
may be lulled into a position of false confidence by the cessation of
drinking and assume there is no need to pay it further attention.
Alternatively he may feel as if he is checking up on the client if he
broaches the subject and be anxious that he will appear moralistic and
punitive. This can lead to inconsistency with the worker vacillating
between overconcern and avoidance. Yet it is important for the worker
to overcome these obstacles because avoidance can serve to reinforce
the belief that drinking problems are a taboo area, whereas the client

needs to be helped to integrate them into his experience.

Conclusion

Underlying this chapter has been the theme that the alcoholic is caught up in a vicious circle. He drinks to escape from difficulties only to find that they are thereby compounded and so necessitate further flight into alcohol. Up to the present time workers too have been ensnared by their own particular vicious circle of avoidance. They have tended to shrink away from working with alcoholics in the belief that specialist skills and expertise are pre-requisites to intervention. Much of the literature and the actual organisation of services have endorsed this view. Difficulties arise when clients present who require help more promptly than would be feasible through normal referral routes, or who do not wish to see a specialist. Helpers are then under pressure to intervene, but have not developed appropriate helping strategies. As alcohol abuse increases as a social problem this predicament becomes more acute. One of the purposes of this chapter has been to delineate the areas in which workers may require specialist knowledge and skills. Equally important has been the attempt to demystify the process of helping the alcoholic and, by illustrating some of the characteristics of the helping process, to identify the ways in which the principles underlying help for other client groups apply with equal validity to the alcoholic and his family.

REFERENCES

Armor, D.J., Polich, J.M. & Stanbul, H.B. (1977) *Alcoholism and Treatment*, The Rand Corporation, Santa Monica, California.

Association of Canadian Distillers (1973) Submission to the Government of Ontario.

Azrin, N.H. (1976) 'Improvements in the community reinforcement approach to alcoholism', *Behaviour Research & Therapy*, 14, pp. 339-48.

Azrin, N.H., Flores, T. & Kaplan, S.J. (1975) 'Job-finding club: a group assisted program for obtaining employment', *Behaviour Research & Therapy*, 13, pp. 17-27.

Bailey, M. (1961) 'Alcoholism and Marriage', *Quarterly Journal of Studies on Alcohol*, 22, pp. 81-97.

Bailey, M.B. (1962) 'Outcomes of alcoholic marriages; endurance, termination or recovery', *Quarterly Journal of Studies on Alcohol*, 23, pp. 610-23.

Bales, R.F. (1959) 'Cultural differences in ideas of alcoholism', in McCarthy, R.G. (ed.), *Drinking and Intoxication*, Free Press, New York.

Bandura, A. (1969) *Principles of Behaviour Modification*, Holt, Reinhart & Winston, New York.

Bernstein, D.A. & Borkovec, T.D. (1973) *Progressive Relaxation Training: A Manual for the Helping Professions*, Research Press, Champaign, Ill.

Blennerhassett, G.B. (1976) *Report of the Departmental Committee on Drinking and Driving*, HMSO, London.

Brain, R. (1961) *Drug Addiction, First Report*, Ministry of Health & Scottish Department of Health, London.

Bruun, K., et al., (1975) *Alcohol Control Policies in Public Health Perspective*, Finnish Foundation for Alcohol Studies, Helsinki.

Cahalan, D. & Cissin, I.H. (1968) 'American Drinking Practices, Survey of Friendship from a National Probability Sample, 1. Extent of Drinking by Population Sub-Groups', *Quarterly Journal of Studies on Alcohol*, 29, p. 142.

Cahalan, D., Cissin, I.H. & Crossley, H.M. (1969) *American Drinking Practices: A national study of drinking behaviour and attitudes. Monograph No. 6*, Rutgers Centre for Alcohol Studies, New Brunswick.

Cahalan, D. & Room, R. (1974) *Problem Drinking Among American Men*, Rugers Centre for Alcohol Studies, New Brunswick.

Cartwright, A.K.J., Shaw, S.J. & Spratley, T.A. (1975) *Designing a Comprehensive Community Response to Problems of Alcohol Abuse*, Report to the Department of Health & Social Security by the Maudsley Alcohol Pilot Project.

Clare, A. (1977) 'How Good is Treatment?' in Edwards, G. & Grant, M. (eds.), *Alcoholism: New Knowledge and New Responses*, Croom Helm, London.

Clarke, W. (1966) 'Operational Definition of Drinking Problems and Associated Prevalence Rates', *Quarterly Journal of Studies on Alcohol*, 27, pp. 648-68.

Clayson, C. (1977) 'The role of licensing law in limiting the misuse of alcohol', in Edwards, G. & Grant, M. (eds.), *Alcoholism: New Knowledge and New Responses*, Croom Helm, London.

Cohen, G. & Collins, M. (1970) 'Alkaloids from catecholamines in adrenal tissues: possible role in alcoholism', *Science*, 167, p. 1,749.

Cork, R.M. (1969) *The Forgotten Children*, Addiction Research Foundation, Toronto.

Costello, R.M. (1973) 'Alcoholism Treatment and Evaluation: in search of methods', *International Journal of Addiction*, 10 (2), pp. 251-75.

Costello, R.M. (1973) 'Alcoholism Treatment and Evaluation: in search of methods, II', *International Journal of Addiction*, 10 (5), pp. 857-76.

Coyle, J. & Fischer, B. (1977) 'A specialised treatment service for young problem drinkers: treatment results obtained during the first six months of the treatment programme', *British Journal of Addiction*, 10 (2),pp. 251-75.

Davies, D.L. (1962) 'Normal Drinking in Recovered Alcohol Addicts', *Quarterly Journal of Studies on Alcohol*, 23, pp. 94-104.

Davies, D.L. (1974) Foreword, in Wilkins, R.H., *The Hidden Alcoholic in General Practice*, Elek Science, London.

Davies, D.L. (1977) 'The Epidemiology of Alcoholism', in Davies, D.L. (ed.), *The Ledermann Curve*, Alcohol Education Centre, London.

Davies, J. & Stacey, B. (1972) *Teenagers and Alcohol: A Developmental Study in Glasgow*, vol. II, HMSO, London.

Davies, M. (1977) *Support Systems in Social Work*, Routledge & Kegan Paul, London.

Davis, V.E. & Walsh, M.J. (1970) 'Alcohol, amines and alkaloids: a possible biological basis for alcohol addiction', *Science*, 167, pp. 1005-7.

Department of Health and Social Security (1973) *Community Services for Alcoholics*, Circular HM 21/73.

Department of Health and Social Security (1975) *Better Services for the Mentally Ill*, Commnd. 6233, HMSO, London.

Department of Health and Social Security (1976) *Prevention and Health: Everybody's Business. A Re-Assessment of Public and Personal Health*, HMSO, London.

Dight, S. (1975) *Scottish Drinking Habits*, Mimeo, Office of Population Censuses & Surveys, London.

Dight, S. (1976) *Scottish Drinking Habits*, Office of Population Censuses & Surveys, Social Survey Division, HMSO, London.

Drewery, J. & Rae, J.B. (1969) 'A group comparison of alcoholic and non-alcoholic marriages using the interpersonal perception technique', *British Journal of Psychiatry*, 115, pp. 287-300.

Duffy, J.C. (1977) 'Estimating the Proportion of Heavy Drinkers', in Davies, D.L., *The Ledermann Curve*, Alcohol Education Centre, London.

Edwards, G., Chandler, J. & Hensman, C. (1972) 'Drinking in a London Suburb. I: Correlates of Normal Drinking', *Quarterly Journal of Studies on Alcohol*, Suppl. 6, pp. 69-93.

Edwards, G., Hawker, A., Hensman, C., Peto, J. & Williamson, V. (1973) 'Alcoholics Known or Unknown to Agencies: Epidemiological studies in a London suburb', *British Journal of Psychiatry*, 123, pp. 169-83.

Edwards, G. (1977) 'The Alcohol Dependence Syndrome: Usefulness of an Idea', in Edwards, G. & Grant, M. (eds.), *Alcoholism: New Knowledge and New Responses*, Croom Helm, London.

Edwards, G. & Grant, M. (1977) *Alcoholism: New Knowledge and New Responses*, Croom Helm, London.

Edwards, G., Gross, M.M. Keller, J. Moser, J. & Room, R. (1977) *Alcohol Related Disabilities*, Offset Publication No. 32, WHO, Geneva.

Edwards, G., & Orford, J. (1977) 'Alcoholism: a controlled trial of treatment and advice', *Journal of Studies on Alcohol*, 38 (5), pp. 1004-31.

Emrick, C.D. (1974) 'A Review of Psychologically Oriented Treatment of Alcoholism, I', *Quarterly Journal of Studies on Alcohol*, 35, pp. 523-49.

Emrick, C.D. (1975) 'A Review of Psychologically Oriented Treatment of Alcoholism, II', Journal of Studies on Alcohol, 36, pp. 88-108.

Family Discussion Bureau (1962) *The Marital Relationship as a Focus for Casework*, Codicote Press.

Field, P.B. (1962) 'A New Cross-Cultural Study of Drunkenness', in Pitman, D.J. & Snyder, C.R. (eds.), *Society, Cultural and Drinking Patterns*, Wiley, New York.

Goodman, G. (1972) *Companionship therapy: studies in structured intimacy*, Jossey-Bass, San Francisco.

Goodwin, D.W. Crane, J.B. & Guze, S.B. (1969) 'Alcoholic Blackouts: a review and clinical study of one hundred alcoholics', *American Journal of Psychiatry*, 126, pp. 191-8.

Grant, M. (1977) 'Access and influence — the implications of professional education for primary and secondary prevention of alcoholism in the general population', *Proceedings of the 23rd International Institute on the Prevention and Treatment of Alcoholism*, ICAA, Lausanne.

Gwinner, P.D.V. (1976) 'The Treatment of Alcoholics in a Military Context', *Journal of Alcoholism*, 11 (1), pp. 24-32.

Gwinner, P.D.V. (1977) 'The Young Alcoholic: Approaches to Treatment', in Madden, J.S., Walker, R. & Kenyon, W.H., *Alcoholism and Drug Dependence: A Multi-Disciplinary Approach*, Plenum, New York.

Hawker, A. (1978) *Adolescents and Alcohol*, Edsall, London.

Hayman, F. (1967) 'The Myth of Social Drinking', *Psychiatric Spectator*, 8, p. 3.

Heath, D.B. (1958) 'Drinking Patterns of the Bolivian Camba', *Quarterly Journal of Studies on Alcohol*, 19, p. 491.

Hollis, F. (1964) *A Psychosocial Therapy*, Random House, New York.

Horton, D. (1943) 'The Functions of Alcohol in Primitive Societies: a cross cultural study', *Quarterly Journal of Studies on Alcohol*, 4, p. 199.

Hunt, G.M. & Azrin, N.H. (1973) 'The community-reinforcement approach to alcoholism', *Behaviour Research & Therapy*, 11, pp. 91-104.

Isbell, H., Fraser, H.F., Wikter, A., Belleville, R.E. & Eisenman, A.J. (1955) 'An experimental study on the aetiology of "rum fits" and delirium tremens', *Quarterly Journal of Studies on Alcohol*, 16, pp. 1-33.

Jackson, J.K. (1954) 'The adjustment of the family to the crisis of alcoholism', *Quarterly Journal of Studies on Alcohol*, 15, pp. 562-86.

Jahoda, G. & Cramond, J. (1972) *Children and alcohol: a develop-*

mental study in Glasgow, Vol. 1, HMSO, London.

Jellinek, E.M. (1960) *The Disease Concept of Alcoholism*, Hillhouse Press, New Brunswick.

Jones, M.C. (1968) 'Personality correlates and antecedents of drinking patterns in adult males', *Journal of Consulting and Clinical Psychology*, 32 (1), pp. 2-12.

Kalant, H. (1975) 'Direct effects of ethanol on the nervous system', *Federation Proceedings*, 34 (10), pp. 1930-41.

Kalb, M. & Propper, M.S. (1976) 'The future of alcohology craft or science?', *American Journal of Psychiatry*, 133 (6), pp. 641-5.

Keller, M. (1970) 'The Great Jewish Drink Mystery, *British Journal of Addiction*, 64, p. 287.

Keller, M. (1976) 'Problems with alcohol: an historical perspective', in Filstead, W.J., Rossi, J.J. & Keller, M. (eds.), *Alcohol and Alcohol Problems: New Thinking and New Directions*, Ballinger, Cambridge, Mass.

Krasner, N. (1977) 'The Reality of Medico Psychiatric Co-operation', in Edwards, G. & Grant, M. (eds.), *Alcoholism: New Knowledge and New Responses*, Croom Helm, London.

Ledermann, S. (1956) *Alcool, Alcoolisme, Alcoolisation*, Institut National d'Etudes Demographiques Cahiers No. 29, Presses Universitaries de France, Paris.

de Lint, J. & Schmidt, W. (1971) 'Consumption averages and alcoholism prevalence: a brief review of epidemiological investigations', *British Journal of Addiction*, 66, pp. 97-107.

Lloyd, R.W. & Salzberg, H.C. (1975) 'Controlled social drinking: an alternative to abstinence as a treatment goal for some alcohol abusers', *Psychological Bulletin*, 87 (6), pp. 815-24.

MacMahon, B. (1967) 'Mental Illness', in Clarke, D.W. & MacMahon, B. (eds.), *Preventive Medicine*, A.J. Churchill, London.

Madden, J.S. (1975) 'Group counselling of alcoholics by a voluntary group', *British Journal of Psychiatry*, 126, pp. 289-91.

Makëla, K. (1975) 'Consumption level and cultural drinking patterns as determinants of alcohol problems', *Journal of Drug Issues*, 5, p. 344.

Malan, D.H. (1963) *A study of brief psychotherapy*, Tavistock Publications, London.

Mandelbaum, D.G. (1962) 'Alcohol and culture', *Current Anthropology*, 6, p. 281.

Matza, D. (1969) *Becoming Deviant*, Prentice Hall, Englewood Cliffs, New Jersey.

McAndrew, C. & Edgerton, R.B. (1970) *Drunken Comportment: A social Explanation*, Nelson, London.

McCord, J., McCord, W. & Thurber, E. (1962) 'Some effects of paternal absence on male children', *Journal of Abnormal Social Psychology*, 64, pp. 361-9.

Mello, N.K. & Mendelson, J.H. (1970) 'Experimentally induced intoxication in alcoholics: a comparison between programmed and spontaneous drinking', *Journal of Pharmacology and Experimental Therapeutics*, 173, pp. 101-16.

Mendelson, J.H. (1964) 'Experimentally induced chronic intoxication and withdrawal in alcoholics', *Quarterly Journal of Studies on Alcohol*, 16, pp. 1-33.

Merseyside, Lancashire & Cheshire Council on Alcoholism (1975) *Alcoholism and its Variations*, 12th Annual Report, Liverpool.

Miller, C.H. & Agnew, N. (1974) 'The Ledermann Model of Alcohol Consumption: description, implications and assessment', *Quarterly Journal of Studies on Alcohol*, 35, pp. 877-98.

Miller, W.R. & Munoz, R.F. (1976) *How to Control Your Drinking*, Prentice-Hall, Englewood Cliffs, New Jersey.

Nichols, B. (1972) *Father Figure: An Uncensored Autobiography*, Heinemann, London.

O'Connor, J. (1978) *The Young Drinkers*, Tavistock, London.

Orford, J., Oppenheimer, E., Egert, S., Hensman, C. & Guthrie, S. (1976) 'The cohesiveness of alcoholism-complicated marriages and it its influence on treatment outcome', *British Journal of Psychiatry*, 128, pp. 318-39.

Parad, H.J. (1965) *Crisis Intervention: Selected Readings*, New York.

Pattison, E.M. (1973) 'Drinking Outcomes of Alcoholism Treatment', in Kessel, N., Hawker, A., & Chalke, H., *Alcoholism: A Medical Profile, Proceedings of the First International Medical Conference on Alcoholism*, Edsall, London.

Pattison, E.M. (1974) 'Rehabilitation of the chronic alcoholic', in Kissin, B. & Begleiter, H. (eds.), *The Biology of Alcoholism*, Vol. 3, *Clinical Pathology*, Plenum Press, New York.

Plant, M.A. (1975) *Drugtakers in an English Town*, Tavistock, London.

Plant, M.A. (1975) 'Occupational factors in alcoholism', in Grant, M. & Kenyon, W.H. (eds.), *Alcoholism in Industry*, Alcohol Education Centre and MLCCA, London.

Plant, M.A. & Pirie, F. 'Self reported alcohol consumption and alcohol-related problems: a study in four Scottish towns' *Social Psychiatry* (in press).

Plaut, T.F. (1967) *Alcohol Problems: A Report to the Nation by the*

Co-Operative Commission on the Study of Alcoholism, Oxford University Press, New York.

Rankin, J.E., Schmidt, W., Popham, R.E. & de Lint, J. (1975) 'Epidemiology of alcoholic liver disease – insights and problems', in Khanna, J.M. *et al.* (eds.), *Alcoholic Liver Pathology*, Alcoholism & Drug Addiction Research Foundation of Ontario, Toronto.

Rapoport, L. (1965) 'State of Crisis: Some Theoretical Considerations', in: Parad, H.J. (ed.), *Crisis Intervention*, Family Service Association of America, New York.

Rapoport, L. (1972) 'Crisis intervention as a mode of brief treatment', in: Roberts, R. & Nee R. (eds), *Introduction to Theories of Social Casework*, University of Chicago.

Rathod, N.H. (1977) 'Making Treatment Better, in Edwards, G. & Grant, M. (eds.) *Alcoholism: New Knowledge and New Responses*, Croom Helm, London.

Ripple, L. (1964) *Motivation, Capacity and Opportunity*, University of Chicago Press.

Roberts, R. & Nee, R. (eds.), (1972) *Introduction to Theories of Social Casework*, University of Chicago.

Robinson, D. (1976) *From Drinking to Alcoholism: A Sociological Commentary*, Wiley, London.

Ron, M.A. (1977) 'Brain damage in chronic alcoholism: a neuropathological, neuroradiological and psychological review', *Psychological Medicine*, 1, pp. 103-12.

Room, R. (1977) 'Measurement and distribution of drink patterns and problems in general populations', in Edwards, G., Gross, M.M., Keller, J., Moser, J. & Room, R., *Alcohol Related Disabilities*, Offset Publication No. 32, WHO, Geneva.

Schmidt, W. (1977) 'Cirrhosis and alcohol consumption: an epidemiological perspective' in Edwards, G. & Grant, M. *Alcoholism: New Knowledge and New Responses*, Croom Helm, London.

Schmidt, W. & de Lint, J. (1972) 'Causes of death in alcoholics', *Quarterly Journal of Studies on Alcohol*, 33 (1),pp. 171-85.

Scottish Health Education Unit (1978) *Understanding Alcohol and Alcoholism in Scotland*, SHEU, Edinburgh.

Semple, B.M. & Yarrow, A. (1974) 'Health education, alcohol and alcoholism in Scotland', *Health Bulletin*, 32.

Shaw, G.K. (1978) 'Alcohol and the central nervous system', *Clinics in Endrocrinology and Metabolism*, 7 (2).

Shields, J. (1977) 'Genetics and Alcoholism', in Edwards, G. & Grant, M. (eds.), *Alcoholism: New Knowledge and New Responses*, Croom

Helm, London.

Shuckit, M.A. & Gunderson, K.E. *Alcoholism in Young Men*, Report No. 75/14, Naval Health Research Centre, San Diego, California.

Sobell, M.B. & Sobell, L.C. (1976) 'Second year treatment outcome of alcoholics treated by individualized behaviour therapy: results', *Behaviour Research & Therapy*, 14, pp. 195-215.

Steiner, C.M. (1969) 'The Alcoholic Game', *Quarterly Journal of Studies on Alcohol*, 30, pp. 920-38.

Steinglass, P., Davis, D.I. & Berenson, D. (1977) 'Observations of conjointly hospitalized alcoholic couples during sobriety and intoxication: implications for theory and therapy', *Family Process*, 16, pp. 1-16.

Sterne, W.S. & Pitman, D.J. (1965) 'The concept of motivation: a source of institutional and professional blockage in the treatment of alcoholics', *Quarterly Journal of Studies on Alcohol*, 26, pp. 44-55.

Sulkunen, P. (1976) 'Drinking patterns and level of alcohol consumption: and international overview', in Gibbins, R.J. *et al.* (eds.), *Research Advances in Drug Problems, Vol. 3*, Wiley, New York.

Thomson, A.D. (1978) 'Alcohol and nutrition', *Clinics in Endrocrinology and Metabolism*, 7 (2).

Tiebout, H.M. (1949) 'The act of surrender in the treatment process with special reference to alcoholism', *Quarterly Journal of Studies on Alcohol*, 10, pp. 48-58.

Trotter, T. (1804) *An Essay on Drunkenness*, Longman, Hurst, Rees & Orme, London.

Truax, C. & Wargo, D. (1966) 'Psychotherapeutic encounters that change behaviour: for better or for worse', *American Journal of Psychotherapy*, 20, pp. 499-520.

Walker, S. (1975) *Learning and Reinforcement*, Methuen, London.

Wexberg, L.E. (1951) 'Alcoholism as a sickness', *Quarterly Journal of Studies on Alcohol*, 12, pp. 217-230.

Whalen, T. (1953) 'Wives of alcoholics: four types observed in a family service agency', *Quarterly Journal of Studies on Alcohol*, 14, pp. 632-41.

Wilson, C. & Orford, J. (1978) 'Children of alcoholics: report of a preliminary study with comments on the literature', *Journal of Studies on Alcohol* (in press).

Wilson, G.B. (1939) *Alcohol and the Nation*, Nicholson & Watson, London.

World Health Organization (1952) *Expert Committee Report, No. 48*, WHO, Geneva.

World Health Organization (1964) *Expert Committee on Mental Health: Technical Report Series, No. 273*, WHO, Geneva.

CONTRIBUTORS

Anthony W. Clare Senior Lecturer, Institute of Psychiatry, University of London

D.L. Davies Medical Director, Alcohol Education Centre, London

Marcus Grant Director, Alcohol Education Centre, London

Paul Gwinner Consultant Psychiatrist, Newington Unit, Ticehurst House, Sussex

Judith Harwin Lecturer in Social Work, London School of Economics

Ray J. Hodgson Senior Lecturer, Addiction Research Unit, Institute of Psychiatry, University of London

Linda Hunt Lecturer in Social Work, University of Manchester

Jim Orford Principal Psychologist, Exe Vale Hospital, Exeter

Martin A. Plant Sociologist, University Department of Psychiatry, Royal Edinburgh Hospital

David Robinson Senior Lecturer in Sociology, Addiction Research Unit, Institute of Psychiatry, University of London

G.K. Shaw Director, Elmdene Alcoholism Unit, Bexley Hospital, Kent.

S.J. Shaw Research Sociologist, Detoxification Evaluation Project, London

INDEX

For Product Safety Concerns and Information please contact our EU
representative GPSR@taylorandfrancis.com
Taylor & Francis Verlag GmbH, Kaufingerstraße 24, 80331 München, Germany